FORCED LANDING!

For two hours Ben worked over the engine. He ripped off the cowling and the carburetor as he sought the source of trouble. The temperature was thirty degrees below zero. . . . Finally they climbed aboard. The engine responded. The two men tensed as the ship left the rough ice and lifted itself into the air.

But they were aloft for only ten minutes when the engine failed again. Once more they brushed close to death as the plane lurched to the uneven ice. Once more Ben sweated over the engine, his finger tips freezing solid.

Then they were aloft again, this time in total darkness when the fuel gave out. For the third time, the plane headed toward the ice below. For twenty minutes it floated downward in the quiet darkness. . . .

WINGS OVER ALASKA
was originally published
by Julian Messner.

Critics' Corner:

"How he triumphs over the dangers of the arctic . . . makes exciting and informative reading for boys who love real stories of real people and adventure."

—Virginia Kirkus Service

"Teen-age adventure enthusiasts will enjoy reading this action-packed story. Particularly engrossing is the plane crash in a blizzard and the seventeen days of wandering before being rescued."

—Chicago School Journal

"The author succeeds very well in showing the successes and failures of the men who wanted to fly . . . the reader learns much about the conditions in Alaska and the difficulties of bad weather. . . . Recommended for high school students, especially those interested in airplanes."

—Diocesan Library Association, Cleveland, Ohio

About the Author:

EDWARD A. HERRON first traveled to Alaska in 1934 just after graduating from St. Joseph's College. Since then he has come to know the forty-ninth state intimately, and two of his children were born there. Mr. Herron has written many popular biographies about the courageous men who came to Alaska to help the raw, uncharted country.

WINGS OVER ALASKA

The Story of
Carl Ben Eielson
Born: July 10, 1897
Died: November 9, 1929

Edward A. Herron

AN ARCHWAY PAPERBACK
WASHINGTON SQUARE PRESS, INC. • NEW YORK

WINGS OVER ALASKA

An Archway Paperback edition

1st printing...................July, 1967
2nd printing...................May, 1968

L

Published by
Washington Square Press, Inc., 630 Fifth Avenue, New York, N.Y.

WASHINGTON SQUARE PRESS editions are distributed in the
U.S. by Simon & Schuster, Inc., 630 Fifth Avenue, New
York, N.Y. 10020 and in Canada by Simon & Schuster
of Canada, Ltd., Richmond Hill, Ontario, Canada.

What sets one man from another for history's accolade? The reasons are generally many, often diverse and sometimes hard to set a finger on. Many men gaze on stars, as did Ben Eielson; few soar so far from the earth, figuratively as well as literally, in questing for a particular star. Ben Eielson reached his, and the light of night shines all the brighter on Alaska because of that.

E. L. BARTLETT
United States Senator
from the state of Alaska

CHAPTER 1

Carl Ben Eielson (pronounced Ileson) stretched out on his bunk. He was long and the bunk was short. His feet dangled in the clear. He was wide-eyed, staring into the darkness. All about him were the night noises of the barracks: the slow, even breathing, the faint snores, the mumbled half-words that escaped from dreams. From outside came the grinding sound of a truck as it labored along the unpaved streets of the hastily constructed camp at Mather Field, near Sacramento, California. Through the open window he could see the dim glow of lights burning at the far side of the base as carpenters rushed other barracks to completion.

It was October, 1918, and the world was at war. Ben studied the dial of his wrist watch. Three o'clock in the morning. With a sudden gesture of impatience, he slipped from the bunk, dressed quietly and, shoes in hand, walked outside the barracks. He sat on the wooden steps, lacing his shoes, looking at the clear white disc of the California moon. He read the signs of the coming weather with satisfaction.

"Shouldn't have any trouble," he whispered. "Shouldn't have the least trouble. Get this flight completed, go down to March Field for advanced training—and four months from now, I'll be in France, fighting over the front lines."

But he could not chase the nervousness that churned in his stomach. "Twenty years old," he whispered as he straightened, "and I act like I'm sixty. It's a wonder the Army even lets me fly an airplane!"

He started walking down the dirt road with a long, swinging stride well in keeping with his tall, lean body. His ancestors had been Norwegian, hardy Norsemen who had first conquered the Atlantic, then plunged westward across America to build homes in the face of blizzards and snowstorms and billowing clouds of dusty North Dakota. But Ben Eielson was a new breed of Norseman. They had conquered the seas. He had his eyes turned toward the sky.

Almost without thought he walked to the long row of hangars silhouetted against the night sky.

"Halt! Who goes there?"

"Cadet Eielson."

"Advance and be recognized."

The sentry waited cautiously, gun poised. He peered into Ben's face. "Oh, it's you, sir." He saluted clumsily. "I guess I should have expected you. Don't you ever sleep like the other cadets?"

Ben shook his head. He held out his hand to the soldier, who was scarcely more than a boy, and walked with him toward the hangars. "Butterflies again, Hank."

"Thought so. What's it this time?"

"Long-distance cross-country flight. Final check-out."

"Well, sir, I've done everything I can. The ship is sure ready." The sentry yawned. "Work all day on the flight line, then pull guard duty at night. Just doesn't seem right."

"Glad to walk your post for you, Hank. I can't sleep a wink."

Hank Robinson shook his head sympathetically. "Like final exams at school, huh, sir?"

Ben nodded. "Worse. Flunk this one, and I might not get another chance to repeat."

"You were late getting in yesterday, sir. Trouble?"

"Got lost. As usual. Lucky I picked up the railroad and came on in. Don't think the instructor noticed."

"Shucks, sir, you won't have trouble tomorrow."

Ben shook his head dolefully. "Hank, I could get lost walking from the barracks to the mess hall."

"Ah, you don't mean that, sir."

"I do. I remember I was about four years old one time back home in North Dakota; the folks sent me out to feed the chickens behind the barn.

3

You know it took them three hours to find me? I almost walked clear out of Traill County before they found me when the moon came up!"

"Sure, sir, but a four-year-old boy! Anybody that age could get lost!"

"I did it when I was fourteen, too. Went hunting with my kid brothers down by the Goose River. I was so busy making turkey tracks so I wouldn't get lost I never fired a shot—and I still got lost. I wandered around all night yelling like a sick cow. If it hadn't been for the Red River blocking my way, I would have walked clear into Minnesota!"

"You're just telling stories, Mr. Eielson. Nothing's going to happen to you tomorrow. You won't get lost."

"Wish you'd tell my stomach that, so I could get a little sleep."

They walked out on the flight line. In the darkness the long line of Curtiss JN-4 training planes looked like grasshoppers with extended wings, waiting for the morning.

"I got to get back to my post," Hank Robinson said. "I know just what you're going to do, sir. You're going to walk down to 56, rub your hands over the prop, kick a little on the wheels and then go back to the barracks and sleep. Just you go right ahead. And good luck with the flight in the morning!"

Ben walked past the shadows cast by the small

ships tethered to the ground. He came to a halt before the plane with the big numerals 56 painted on the fuselage just aft of the two open cockpits. The longer upper wing spread forty-three feet in the air above his head, secured to its lower, shorter mate by an intricate rigging of spars and wires. From the blunt-nosed motor to the thin tail skid, the plane was only twenty-four feet in length. With its stilled propeller horizontal to the ground, it had the appearance of a drowsy animal. The thin bicycle tires of the landing gear seemed to bend in slightly as though they, too, were resting for the night.

He rubbed affectionately on the prop, looking self-consciously over his shoulder to see if his mechanic was watching from the sentry box. He kicked gently at the undercarriage. Then, with an easy, vaulting step, he climbed into the rear cockpit.

The fingers of his right hand curled gently around the stick. His feet moved instinctively on the rudder bar. He felt his nervousness ebbing away. He slumped far down in the seat until his head was resting on the padded cushion surrounding the cockpit. He blinked his eyes once, twice, then they closed, and he drifted off to sleep.

At noon the next day a small airplane droned over the crowded streets of Oakland. There was something odd and persistent about the noise of the churning motor, as though it kept asking a question. People in the streets watched curiously, for airplanes were a rarity.

"He's lost," someone said.

"He's trying to land."

"He's just one of them crazy fliers trying to show off."

But the plane twisted and turned, ignoring the white dots of upturned faces. It swerved from San Francisco Bay on the west side of the city to San Pablo Bay to the north. It seemed to waver over the myriad of railroad tracks forming a network within the city. Finally, the motor coughed and was silent. The dipping wings straightened. The blunt nose of the plane slanted down an imaginary inclined track toward a farm on the southern edge of the city. The airplane came in fast, its wings outstretched as though asking for help. It skimmed past a clump of swaying eucalyptus trees. The wheels touched the rutted earth. The plane bounced, settled, then the ship rolled forward crazily until it came to a full stop.

A farmer came running over the fields, stopping every few minutes to look in horror at the red mesh of ruined tomatoes.

The aviator, wrapped in a leather jacket, pushed a pair of goggles high on his forehead, uncoiled from the narrow cockpit and started to climb down from the wing of the airplane. "Is that the city of San Jose?" he called over his shoulder.

"Now . . . now . . . don't you make another move, mister. I got you covered." The farmer seized a shovel, balanced it in his hands and advanced.

The aviator retreated hastily. "What's wrong? All I want to know is . . ."

"Don't you say a word. I heard about them German submarines off the Marin Peninsula, launching airplanes that come in and snoop and spy. Why, you even talk like a foreigner, you do."

"Foreigner?" The aviator exploded. "Where'd you think I got this airplane? Look!" The angry young man pointed to the insignia UNITED STATES ARMY painted on the side of the plane.

The farmer lowered his shovel. He looked all around the plane, bending to untangle a great mass of tomato vines hooked onto the tail skid. The young man jumped to the ground.

"Well, now," the farmer said hesitantly, "maybe I did make a mistake. I just kind of thought . . ."

"Bet your boots you made a mistake—calling me a foreigner, holding me up with a shovel just like I was a—"

"Now, son," the farmer said firmly, "just cool down under that collar of yours. Nobody asked you to come down out of the sky. Nobody asked you to mess up ten dollars' worth of tomatoes. And when it comes to making mistakes—did I hear you mention something about San Jose?"

"Yes. I'm flying from Sacramento to Santa Cruz on a training flight, and I ran out of gas. I thought maybe . . ."

"You can think a lot, mister, especially if you think this is San Jose. Just Oakland, that's all. Maybe forty miles off your course. Little more, little less."

"Oakland? That's impossible!" The aviator flushed. The crimson tide started low on his long neck and flowed upward over his cheeks until his face was fiery red. Then he grinned sheepishly. "To tell the truth, the map I was using was blown out of the cockpit. I must have switched railroads—I mean, the tracks I was following from the air." He slapped his hand hard against the plane. "Gosh, what a flier I am! I'll be a big help over in France! Probably fly backward and land in England!"

"Now, then, son," the farmer said consolingly, "don't you worry. You're not the only one gets mixed up. I can get lost driving a team of horses up to market on a foggy morning. Can't help you to get down to Santa Cruz, but I'll help you get that plane up in the sky again. You need gasoline?"

"I sure do. That tank is bone-dry."

"Just so happens my son-in-law bought himself an automobile last month and we got three drums of gasoline up by the barn. Whyn't you come on up to the house and rest a spell? What's your name, son?"

"Eielson. Carl Ben Eielson. My friends call me Ben."

"Well, come along, Ben. My name's Harvey Thomas. Got a boy over in France just about your age. Plenty worried about him, too. He's in the Battle of the Marne that they're fighting right now. Infantry."

Harvey Thomas led the way over the rows of tomato plants to the small farmhouse set in the grove of eucalyptus trees. He walked to the red barn, threw wide the door and pointed to a black, shining Ford . . . "There she is," he said proudly. "Beauty, isn't she?"

"Uh-huh. My dad's got one. Back home in Hatton, North Dakota. That's how I started thinking of flying—fooling around with Dad's car."

"Doesn't affect my son-in-law that way. Bert says he wouldn't go up in an airplane for a whole tomato patch full of dollar bills. Say, Ben, what's it feel like?"

"What?"

"Being up in an airplane like that—floating around, just ducking in and out of them clouds?"

Ben looked at the palm of his opened right hand before replying. "It's great," he said quietly. "Best feeling I ever had in my life. That is," he added hastily, "if your motor keeps turning over and you know where you are!"

Harvey Thomas looked quizzically at Carl Ben Eielson. He placed his finger alongside his long, angular nose. "You been lost before, ain't you, son?"

"Uh-huh."

"Have any trouble with your boss, I mean, with them generals?"

Ben Eielson jammed his flying cap into his hip pocket. He nodded his head. "I sure have. Plenty. They don't think I'm going to do much to win the war." He walked out of the shade of the barn and into the bright sunlight, squinting up into the sky. "I can fly fine," he said seriously. He pointed to the airplane sitting in the tomato field. "I can take up one of those Jennies blindfolded. I can climb almost straight up. Well, nearly. Two thousand feet in ten minutes. I've sideslipped this plane into fields that weren't long enough for an old horse to get his wind up. I've lifted out of places where the ship had to climb almost straight on its tail to clear trees all around. But . . ."

"But you get lost, huh?" Harvey Thomas asked the question with a note of sympathy.

Ben nodded. "Like today. I said the wind blew the map out of the cockpit, and it did—but I sort of helped it go. Wasn't doing me any good. Right after I flew into a heap of clouds and lost contact with the ground, I was clear gone. Picked up the first railroad tracks I saw and followed them to some mountains—and I knew I was lost. So I brought the ship around and flew west, hoping I'd pick up the Pacific Ocean. Had a hard job finding it —that's how bad I am. Then I got mad and just kept flying until my gas ran out—and the motor conked."

"You're in the wrong business, Ben, getting mad when you're a mile high in the sky. Lot safer if you just drove automobiles and got mad on the ground."

"I want to fly," Ben said stubbornly. "I don't want anything else. I just want to fly airplanes."

"Well, I'm not your father to say what you should do and shouldn't do. Come along. We'll start hauling gasoline out to that airplane of yours. I'll drive the wagon around and we'll fill up these oil cans."

Ben pointed overhead to the wire leading to the farmhouse. "You have a telephone?"

"Why, sure," Harvey said proudly. "Just about got everything modern there is. This time next year we aim to get electricity. Just about the first farmhouse in Alameda County, too. Might get our pictures in the paper."

"Would you let me call the field? It's regulation, you know, when we make a forced landing."

11

Harvey scratched his cheek dubiously.

"I'll pay for the call, of course," Ben added hastily, "and for the gasoline, and—and the tomatoes."

"Well, then, just go right ahead and call the Army. We can't have them wondering where you and the airplane are hiding out. Just go right ahead, Ben. Through that screen door and on your right. Telephone's on the wall."

Ben put through the call to the field.

"Captain Plummer, please. Hello, Captain Plummer? This is Cadet Eielson. I ran out of gas, sir. I made an emergency landing at a farm just south of Oakland. Yes, sir, I said Oakland. The plane is in good shape, no damage. Yes, sir, there's gasoline available. We're filling the tanks right now. Yes, sir."

There was a pause, and Ben listened to the loud sounds coming through the earpiece. Once again the scarlet coloring formed low on his neck, climbed over his cheekbones and spread across his forehead. "Very well, sir," he said dejectedly when the tirade had ended, "I'll do as you order, sir."

He hung up the receiver and turned around to Harvey Thomas. His fists were clenched. "They don't trust me to fly the plane back to Mather Field. They're sending an instructor to take it home. I'm to return to the base on the first train."

He walked hastily from the farmhouse and strode down to the airplane. He leaned against the wings and covered his eyes. He didn't want anyone to be watching him.

CHAPTER 2

"Cadet Eielson," the commanding officer said seriously, "some men are never able to fly." He cupped his hands and looked down at them as though he were peering into a well. "Temperamental unfitness, nervousness or some physical defect." He shook his head. "None of these apply to you. You're as steady as a rock. You learned to fly quickly. But, blast it, Eielson," the officer roared, striking his desk a mighty blow with his clenched fist, "you can't read a map—and you can't find your way across a crowded room without getting lost."

"Yes, sir," Ben admitted.

"Eielson," the officer said, rising to his feet and walking around the desk to stand by Ben's side, "in a few months your group is scheduled to be commissioned as second lieutenants in the Aviation

Section, United States Army Signal Corps. By next spring you'll be sent overseas for indoctrination with the French fighter planes, the Spads. Now tell me," he demanded, his head close to Ben's, "what good is a pilot who gets lost and runs out of gas behind the enemy's line? It's happened. Not once, but many times. And frankly, mister, the Army isn't inclined to spend a fortune training a flier, then have him and his ship sit out the war in an enemy prison camp just because he couldn't tell a railroad track from a river when he was four thousand feet in the air!"

The color ebbed from Ben's tanned face. This was no ordinary reprimand from the Commanding Officer. It was a prelude to the words he dreaded— dismissal as an air cadet.

The officer studied the floor intently. Then he went back to his desk, sat down and looked squarely at Ben Eielson. "The country needs every flier it can possibly obtain. It needs you, Eielson." He flipped open a book in front of him and made some notations. "I'm going to leave you alone for the next ten days. That plane 56 is yours. Take it up every hour of the day or night, if you wish, or don't take it up at all. You have my permission to fly from here to China. You can be away from the field as long as you wish—you and the airplane. Only remember this," he continued, leveling his finger at Ben, "ten days from today you'll be checked out on a long-distance cross-country flight. I don't have to tell you what will depend on the outcome. Good day, sir."

Ben saluted. He turned and left the office, his ears still ringing with the biting words of the officer.

He walked to the barracks and started to pack his traveling bag. Better to walk out, to resign now without waiting for further humiliation. Within an hour he could be enlisted in the infantry, and on his way to the fighting in France. There a man didn't have to follow maps. Just fight.

The drone of circling planes filled the air, filtered through the open barracks window. He looked out, eyes to the sky. His heart leaped as he saw the ships of his classmates wheeling below the white clouds. He knew then that he couldn't walk out. "I'll stay," he whispered. "I'll stay until they escort me to the front gate and tell me to go home."

He walked into the hot sun, down to the hangars that seemed to crouch low in the heat. Hank Robinson stood in the shade, looking critically at a snapped piston rod. "Fill the tanks in 56," Ben called to the little mechanic. "I'm taking off in ten minutes."

He checked his simple instrument panel with its compass, fuel gauge and oil-pressure indicator, then he took the plane off with a rush. He checked the compass again while he was still over the field. He climbed for altitude, set his course due west and unrolled the strip map.

Ben figured his speed, which was close to eighty miles an hour, checking a half-hour distance on the map. He marked ten-mile points. He was nervous and his head was never still, twisting from map to compass to the ground objects far below. He checked the roads, the plowed fields, the barns, houses, the odd formation of trees, the flat sheen of rivers, the double shadows of bridges, the serpentine twist of railroad tracks. Always he looked at his watch, counting the minutes.

At the end of the half-hour period he was ten miles short of his penciled check point on the map. He knew then that he must allow for the head wind that was pushing against the plane. He marked his map again, checking his probable point in half an hour's time, and bored northward.

His head was turning endlessly. He looked from map to compass to watch, and downward past the lower wing. He searched for a meeting of two small rivers, thin blue lines that should be outlined sharply against the brown of dry pasture land. His heart sank, for he was unable to see the twisting waterways. Then he looked past the radiator cap in the nose, saw his check point—and his heart soared. He opened his mouth wide and yelled in exultation above the steady roar of the motor.

At the end of the hour, he circled the cone of

the small hill that was his objective, then reversed his course. This time he flew without the map, picking up one check point after the other, calling each aloud unashamedly like a schoolboy chanting from a lesson book. Far ahead he saw the flat expanse of Mather Field beyond Sacramento, the planes clustered about the runways, the long, low hangars with the dark shadows where the doors were wide. He put the ship into a glide, slowed to forty-five miles an hour and landed. He taxied to a halt before the ground crew. Hank Robinson came running over.

"Fill the gas tanks," Ben said. "I'm going up again."

"Sir, you've been gone two hours. Aren't you going to get out and stretch your legs?"

"Fill 'em up."

He took off again, this time flying to the east. He forced himself to call out every check point as it flowed beneath the lower wing of the plane. He held a conversation with himself, shouting above the roar of the motor, identifying every crossroad, dried-up creek bed, railroad spur and bridge.

At his check point he banked sharply and swept off on the top leg of a wide triangle that brought him back to the field over strange territory, calling for his alertness with every passing minute. His tanks were perilously empty, but his confidence unshaken. He beelined to the field and taxied to a halt.

His face was raw from the continual bite of the wind in the open cockpit, but once more he called for gas and took off without resting. When he reached behind him he found a paper bag crammed with sandwiches that Hank Robinson had thrust into the cockpit.

He flew until he was exhausted, until he was chattering with the cold that came with the screaming wind. He was burned from the sun and the wind, wet from the rain—and thirsty. But he kept flying. When dusk was closing with a rush, he returned to the field, coming in on a steep sideslip, fishtailing to kill speed. But the plane struck hard and sheared a wheel. The ship screamed to a halt, tail high in the air. Ben clambered to the ground and crouched on his knees, fingering the crushed undercarriage. Hank Robinson came running up.

"You all right, sir?"

Ben nodded. He pointed to the wreckage. "How soon can we replace that undercarriage?"

"Oh," Hank answered while he tugged at his ear reflectively, "if I order up the parts first thing in the morning, get some of the other mechanics to help, might be tomorrow afternoon, maybe noontime."

"Order the parts out right now. I'll work on it myself during the night."

"You? You can't do that, sir. Even if you could —you haven't had any sleep or food or—anything!"

"You heard me. Order out what you need. That undercarriage is going to be fixed by sunup tomorrow. If it isn't, I'll take the ship up on skids."

Hank lifted his head in admiration. "You really mean that, don't you, sir?"

"Never meant anything more in my life." Ben walked off toward the hangar. Once he looked back. Hank Robinson and his crew were already swarming over 56.

Ben worked through the night with the line crew. At two in the morning, at Hank's insistence he went inside the hangar, stretched across two motor crates and fell alseep.

The sun was barely showing in the east when the crew swung the ship into the wind, and Ben settled himself into the cockpit. He took a last deep drink of the steaming hot coffee handed up to him. Then he nodded to Hank Robinson who chinned himself on the propeller.

Ben listened to the deep, guttural roar of the motor. He looked over at Hank who nodded in approval of the ninety-horsepower OX-5 engine. Then Ben opened the throttle gradually. He settled in his seat as the plane rolled forward, gathering speed. He felt the tail lifting as he pushed the stick forward. Gently he pulled backward. He could feel the sturdy wings responding as they swelled with the buoyancy of the rushing air. He sensed the pressure of the stick on the palm of his hand. The Jenny was airborne.

He leveled off, nursing the motor until the ship had picked up speed. Then he started a gradual climb to the altitude he had selected. He unrolled the strip map and marked his course.

That second day he was in the air for fourteen hours. And the day after, and the day after that. He treated himself with greater harshness than any of the instructors who had been with him since the day he had been sworn into the Army as an air cadet.

Satisfied that the motor was turning perfectly, Ben gave his mind and eyes over to the one exacting chore, matching flight lines on the map with the thousand details that swam lazily beneath the lower wing of the plane.

On each flight he pushed farther and farther from the base. He dropped the ship into flat pastures he had selected beforehand, obtaining gasoline from astonished farmers who welcomed the stranger from the skies. He memorized the entire area for a huge hundred-mile circle about the base. Then he leaped farther outward on long cross-country flights. He was gone from the field for two nights, covering a vast triangle that carried him over tremendous areas of mountain and desert he had never before seen from the air. He became one with the maps, the fuel gauge, the compass, his wrist watch and the earth floating beneath the throbbing plane.

In the long hours aloft, the tenseness began to ebb from him. Secretly he marveled when he saw that some of the navigation moves were becoming almost second nature, accomplished without apparent thought.

He began to trust his senses more and more. His eyes became acutely conscious of depth perception in landings, in judging the degree of the bank as the ship rolled in a turn. His hand upon the stick was light and sure, giving just the right pressure to combat the wayward drift of the plane as it fell off from the head winds. Deep within him muscles reacted to tell Ben when there was a change of altitude or speed. And his ears were keener now than ever before, alert to increased speed of the spinning prop, and wary of vibrations that would portend trouble.

He was able to sit back for longer and longer periods, his head pulled out of the biting slip stream. He was confident of his motor, his plane, of himself and of his position.

Droning high in the sky, he was able to think of his home in Hatton, North Dakota. He had spent his boyhood in a tight family group that included his older sister Elma, and the younger children Adeline, Oliver, Arthur, Helen and Hannah. Life had been exciting in the big white house until tragedy struck with the death of his mother when Ben was fourteen.

Ben had gone out on the wooden porch steps, sat in the darkness and wept. And his father Ole Eielson had sat beside him and shared his tears.

Airplanes? They had meant little to a boy running barefoot through the dirt streets of Hatton. Automobiles were far more exciting—and more and more you could see them chugging up to the homes of the prosperous folks about Hatton.

Ben checked his position carefully before he let his thoughts wander again. Why, yes, it was an airplane flight that first lifted him from the deep grief into which his mother's death had plunged him.

Olava Eielson died in July, 1911. Less than two months later the entire country, and Ben with them, kept up with the day-by-day progress of Calbraith P. Rodgers as the daring aviator flew a frail airplane from New York to California in forty-nine days, the first transcontinental flight.

But it was still automobiles, more than airplanes, that held his fancy when he entered the University of North Dakota in 1914. He had borrowed his father's Ford for the thirty-mile drive over to Grand Forks, and set off in a mist of tearful farewells from his older sister Elma, and boisterous shouts from the young ones clustered about. Ben had bumped grandly over the rutted roads, then succumbed to the lure of the unknown and attempted a short cut over a back road.

He became lost—utterly and completely lost. For two hours he drove about from one unmarked country lane to another, until he came entirely by chance back to Hatton again. He slumped low behind the wheel, hoping he could slip through the town unrecognized. He drove on and on, looking neither to the right nor to the left—then when he was safely past his home town, he shamefacedly scolded himself. "Stick to the road, Ben Eielson," he muttered, "stick to the road or you'll get lost so bad the college year will be finished before you get to Grand Forks!"

The war in Europe was already started, but that was more than four thousand miles away. Being fought between strange countries, it meant little to the tall, gangling boy from Hatton who had become immersed in exciting studies, sports and new friendships. To everything he gave a tremendous drive of restless energy, a trait that would follow him through the remainder of his life.

The rumble of war grew louder, even though it was still being fought so far way. In student discussions the conversation turned to the new breed of soldiers who were coming to the fore—airmen who fought high in the clear blue sky over the earthbound foot soldiers who were dying desperately in the mud of France.

A restlessness was beginning to spread through most of the college students. Suddenly, at the beginning of his third year of college in September, 1916, Ben transferred to the University of Wisconsin, attracted by the bright luster of the law school on the campus at Madison.

The war in Europe suddenly spread and became a world war. Europe's war was America's war. And the churning restlessness of a youth of twenty could be satisfied in only one way—by enlistment.

The United States entered the war in April, 1917. A full nine months passed before Ben was able to overcome the objections of his father and obtain his consent to enlist in the Aviation Section of the Army Signal Corps. And another five frustrating months passed before he was ordered to report for active duty on June 8, 1918.

He was fretfully sure that the war would be over before he had a chance for combat flying.

"I just don't want to go slogging around in the mud of France with the rest of the foot soldiers," he told his friends as they swung on board trains and headed for infantry camps.

Finally it was his turn to board a train heading west to California and the School of Military Aeronautics at Berkeley where he joined eight hundred and fifty other air cadets for an intensive eight weeks of schooling prior to the start of flight training.

When the United States entered the war, it had

only twenty-eight planes and thirty-five trained pilots in the Air Corps. Seventeen months later twelve thousand pilots and six hundred air cadets were using eighty-five hundred planes for basic training before going overseas.

They were no ordinary men who answered the call for enlistment as air cadets. The scrawny Curtiss biplanes with their wired wings, open cockpits and cloth-covered fuselages were just two jumps ahead of the freak stage. There were no parachutes. There was little experience for anyone to fall back on. More students and instructors were killed during training than in the dogfights over the front lines of France.

Yet out of that wild, mushrooming growth of less than a year and a half came a parade of heroes who molded the future aviation history of America.

Carl Ben Eielson was destined to be one of them.

For ten days during his trial period, he flew without faltering. On the ninth day, he had mastered his weakness. Almost imperceptibly he acquired a feel for distances, proportions and speed while viewing the sweep of terrain that rushed in from the horizon and flowed back under the stubby tail of the plane. It became instinctive for him to allow for the wind, to check the ground speed against elasped time for a definite fix on the map and to keep rigidly close to a compass course within a few degrees.

The night before his final check flight down the San Joaquin Valley, he was seized by the intense nervousness that he was to know before every eventful flight. It became impossible for him to sleep. He sat upright in his bunk, staring off into the darkness; then, in despair, he dressed and walked to the flight line. He saw a form, huddled in blankets, asleep under the ship. Ben smiled in gratitude. Hank Robinson. The sight of the little mechanic— and of 56, sturdy in the darkness—calmed him. He returned to the barracks and slept soundly.

Fifteen minutes after he had lifted his ship into the air on his final checkout, he was in trouble. Great billowing rain clouds swept down from the north as though in pursuit of the tiny ship bouncing in the sky. Ben lifted the nose of the plane and tried to fly over the clouds. He flinched when vicious tongues of lightning ripped out and stabbed at the intruding plane. He suffered a wave of panic when the earth disappeared, and he was alone in a roaring, thunderous world of black storm clouds.

With all his heart he wanted to roll over, point downward and streak for the earth, regardless of the depth of the storm clouds, hoping frantically that a few hundred feet of open space would be available so that he could stay in contact with the friendly ground.

But he fought the temptation. He fought the rising panic. He fought the feeling that death was riding alongside the ship in the boiling black thunderheads. He knew that mountains loomed to the east. He knew that he might be within minutes of death.

He trusted his compass implicitly. He was judging his speed from previous timing checks; he had calculated his drift before the storm had overtaken him, and was thoroughly schooled in all the details of deviation that meant success or failure in air navigation.

He held true to his course.

At the end of the time period, he pushed the nose of the plane downward. The wind whistled through the guy wires. At two thousand feet the storm clouds began to thin. At fifteen hundred feet he broke into the clear. He looked over his left wing and grinned. His check point, the junction of two railroads, was immediately below.

When he returned to the field, his instructor grunted in satisfaction and turned away. Hank rushed up and held out his greasy hand in congratulation. And that was the end of the ceremony. He had had his ten days of trial and he'd made it. He was in.

One month later, when Ben returned to the field after a flight that had taken him far over the Mojave Desert, he saw a long line of enlisted men dancing around on the runway. He buzzed the field, climbed and circled, waiting for the soldiers to clear the runway. When he saw them wind back to the barracks, still gyrating like a group of students after a football victory, he swooped in, settled quickly and taxied to the squat hangar.

He was still looking about in bewilderment when Hank Robinson came racing through the empty hangar.

"Mr. Eielson! Mr. Eielson! It's all over!"

"What are you talking about?"

"The war! It's all over. The Armistice has been signed!"

CHAPTER 3

Ben's mind was whirling. He stood with one leg thrown over the cowling. "I've been so busy flying," he said, "I just didn't . . ." He straightened quickly. "Well, thank goodness, it's over. Nobody else can get hurt."

Hank Robinson looked about. Far off in the distance they could hear the shouts of the dancing soldiers. Someone had started a bonfire on the parade grounds, and the red shadows began to leap in the air. "Can't seem to get it through my head. No more war. Thought you and I would be over in France right after Christmas."

"Well . . ." Ben fumbled for words. All he could think of was that his flying career was finished. And he hated himself for being selfish. "You go on up with the fellows, Hank. I'll take care of the plane."

He remained at Mather Field until the tenth of January in 1919 when he was transferred down to March Field at Riverside, California. During the war March Field had been a busy flying-training station equipped with nearly a score of wood and steel hangars, machine shops, repair shops, foundry and finishing shops, oil and gas stations and a gunnery range. There was still flying activity, but the excitement was gone. Everyone about the base had an air of waiting, of counting the days till the end. Flying time for the young student pilots was strictly curtailed, and Ben spent more time in the swimming pool than he did at the controls of his plane.

On the fourth of March, 1919, he was commissioned a second lieutenant, Aviation Section, Signal Officers' Reserve Corps, and honorably discharged.

Already carpenters were boarding up the windows of the barracks. Weeds were beginning to sprout through the cracks in the wooden sidewalks.

The streets had a dusty, unused appearance. A few hours before, Ben had peered into the gloom of the hangars, saddened by the sight of the planes crammed inside like sardines. Outside on the flight lines, dull and lifeless, scores of other planes drooped in the sun.

"Not exactly cheerful, is it, sir?"

Ben turned his head to look at Hank. The mechanic, who stood a full five feet, four inches tall, was preening self-consciously in a checkered black-and-brown suit. A stiff new cap was perched on the bushy, jet-black hair. Ben put his hand on Hank's shoulder. "Don't call me 'sir' any more, just Ben. Ben Eielson. What are your plans?"

Hank straightened importantly. "I'm staying with aviation, Ben. Circus I know back in Minnesota, they got an airplane. Stunt flier. They want me to come and keep the motor running. Just like I did here."

"Good. Maybe I'll run into you out there." But he was just making talk, for he never expected to see the little mechanic again.

Still in a state of bewilderment at the abrupt change in his plans, and no longer interested in the law course he had been pursuing at Wisconsin, he enrolled again in the University of North Dakota. But the textbooks he held in his hand seemed as though they were printed in a foreign language. He could not keep his thoughts on his studies. At night he walked alone on the campus and looked beyond the gaunt trees, and whispered the words that kept repeating themselves in his mind: "I want to fly."

He received a letter from Hank Robinson that had been posted in southern California. "I sure get around in the circus business. I keep two of these Jennies flying every day. You should see what these old planes can do! The Air Corps could learn something watching these stunt men."

The letter only heightened the restlessness that was holding Ben. He went home to his father one weekend and spoke to him of his continued interest in flying.

Ole Eielson shook his head. "Ben, I worried about you all the time you were with the Army. I didn't want you to fly. I don't want you to fly now. I can't think of you up in that sky without thinking someday the motor is going to stop—and you'll fall. But Ben—"

"Yes, Dad."

"You're young, and I'm not going to stop you."

Ben returned to the university, and when the restlessness still held he spoke to one of his professors about it.

"You are not alone, Eielson. It's a natural aftermath of war. As time passes, very likely you will get over it. If not—" The professor lifted his shoulders.

"Suppose I don't get over it?"

"Why not get an airplane and fly? It isn't impossible. I have heard of flying clubs, where several people share the costs—why not you, Eielson? A lot of people want to fly—just need someone like you to show them how."

Ben approached a group of businessmen in Hatton. He was nervous as he looked at the dark-suited men regarding him quizzically. Then he used the eloquence that had gained him brief stardom in college debating circles. "Gentlemen," he said earnestly, "we've entered a new era in America. People are going to fly. Not just aviators—all the people. The Government has eight thousand Curtiss Jennies in storage it wants to sell cheap. Let's buy a Jenny! They're good planes, sturdy planes. I know. I can teach some of you to fly. I can carry others on business trips and pleasure trips."

The businessmen listened, asked questions of the tall young man standing before them, then decided to form a flying club. Quickly they subscribed to the price of a plane.

Over the skies of Hatton a Curtiss JN-4 roared into the air with Ben Eielson at the controls. In his exultation, he whipped the sturdy little biplane into wingovers, loops, Immelmann turns and outside loops. For the benefit of the stockholders of the flying club, openmouthed in the pasture below, he did half rolls, snap rolls, slow rolls and rolling "eights." The brush of the wind on his cheeks brought new life back to his body. He was living again.

Patiently he gave flying instructions to the new owners, fighting the controls when the club members, suddenly terrified, longed for land and took a short cut, nose-diving to the pasture below. He flew off to college in the perky Jenny, trying fruitlessly to keep his mind on his textbooks, always looking through windows to check flying conditions, and completing mental problems in navigation.

There was a telegram from Salt Lake City. MY BOSS CRACKED UP STUNTING YESTERDAY. YOU WANT HIS JOB? HANK ROBINSON.

He resisted the temptation and went back to his studies, but late in the spring when he had closed his books, he joined Hank Robinson and a band of air gypsies making a tour of the county fairs.

"Now, Ben," the little fellow said importantly, "all you have to do is fly your ship. The rest of us do the work."

"Are you my mechanic?"

"Mechanic?" Hank looked at him with a pained expression. "Ben, I graduated. You just wait and see."

The next day at noon when Ben lifted a battered Jenny into the air accompanied by the noise of blaring bands at the State Fair, little Hank Robinson was sitting nonchalantly on the right wing. While Ben circled in full view of the packed grandstand, Hank proceeded to walk on the wings, hang by his heels from the struts, clamber down a trapeze that hung from the undercarriage and swing back and forth, urged on by the cheers of the thousands below. For a full fifteen minutes he performed hair-raising antics, never more than a foot from certain death. Then he clambered into the open cockpit and yelled into Ben's ear, "All right! It's your turn! Give them a thrill down there! Let's see you tear the wings off this ship!"

Even Ben marveled at the punishment the little Jenny took as he whipped around in an endless series of dips and loops. He flipped the ship on its back and dove straight down to the pitcher's box before the grandstand, then pulled out in a screaming arc that barely cleared the green roofs below him.

All through the summer of 1921 the two performed in daredevil exhibitions with a reckless disregard for their lives. Ben graduated to the stage where he was racing with automobiles along country roads, hovering directly above the cars while Hank nonchalantly slipped from plane to auto and back to the plane again.

The two flew every day regardless of the weather. To Ben, flying became second nature. He knew the topography of the Middle West intimately as he followed railroads, rivers, highways and creek beds from one county fair to another. When money came in freely, they slept in the best hotels. When it grew scarce, they rolled in blankets under the ship and looked up at the stars before falling asleep.

Ben lived only for flying. Looking critically at the small gas tanks on the Curtiss plane, he wondered what the sturdy ship could do if it were crammed with gas tanks, and headed eastward to Chicago or New York, or pointed westward to San Francisco and Los Angeles.

"Hank," he called across the hotel room one night, "why can't we plan a long-distance flight?"

"Forget it, Ben. There's no money in it. We'll stick to the flying circus."

"No money? Ross got a check for ten thousand pounds—maybe fifty thousand dollars—flying from England to Australia. And Raymond Orteig is offering twenty-five thousand dollars for the first nonstop flight from New York to Paris. Somebody's got to win it."

"Forget it, Ben. That's dream stuff. We're working men."

In between engagements at the different fairgrounds, they flew the Jenny low over the towns, using the roaring motor to attract attention. They set the plane down in the nearest pasture. When the townspeople came running, Hank seized a megaphone and bellowed, "Step right up, folks, and get yourself a real ride in a real airplane! See your city from the air! Fly over your home! All of America is flying these days. Why don't you? Five dollars, five minutes! Step right up! Line forms on the right!"

But even as he lifted the frightened passengers aloft for their first ride, Ben was looking ahead, his mind far away. He was beginning to dream of the time when passenger planes would carve new pathways in the air.

"Hank," Ben said patiently, while they relaxed one night beside the plane, "maybe we're going at this the wrong way. Stunt flying can't go on forever. Someday that motor's going to miss at the wrong moment, and you and I will be out of business."

"Bad luck to talk that way, Ben," Hank cautioned.

"But sensible. I've been reading the papers. They've started a scheduled airline between Florida and Havana. Over in Paris they're flying passengers between Paris and London. Even the Germans have started airlines out of Berlin. I tell you, Hank, we should think of making flying a career—not just a thrill."

Ben waited for an answer, but all he heard was

a gentle snore. He rolled up in his blankets, propped his head against the undercarriage and fell asleep.

On July 25, 1921, the two buzzed the town of Portal, North Dakota, hoping to stir up some passenger-carrying business. From the air the town seemed asleep although it was barely noon. Instead of the usual wide-flung doors, and people rushing out into the middle of the street to turn white faces skyward, the little plane was totally ignored. Hank jabbed his finger downward, pointing to a level field ringed with spectators. "Must've known we're coming!" he screamed. "Man, we'll make a fortune!"

Ben put on a little show to whet the appetites of the spectators. He did a few death dips, rollovers and loops, then came in low over the treetops, landed smartly and swung the tail of the Jenny with a flourish. A vast cloud of dust swirled back over the crowd. Hank leaped out of the cockpit, flicked some grease from the coveralls which they wore constantly, then lifted his megaphone, ready to entice the customers. A bull-necked army sergeant came striding through the dust, his fists clenched. He seized Hank around the collar.

"I'll give you five seconds to get this egg crate out of the way. We've got some real planes coming in, not a bunch of flying jackasses. Get moving!"

Ben's big, broad mouth set in a straight line. But beyond the sergeant he saw a detachment of troops.

In front of the crowd were army officers, the sun glinting on their gold insignia. "Hank," he called, "I'll taxi down to the far end of the field and walk back. Wait here for me."

After he had parked the plane, he shed his flying jacket and goggles. The remark of the army sergeant still rankled. He found Hank bristling with excitement.

"It's those four army planes, the Black Wolf Squadron, flying from New York up to Alaska, Ben! They're going to land here any minute! Four De Havillands. And the commanding officer is Captain Streett. Remember him?"

Ben nodded. "I've been reading about it in the papers. First flight from the States up to Alaska. Who's the brass over there?" He motioned to the line of officers who looked toward the sky.

"Don't know. From headquarters in Washington, I guess. From here the planes fly into Canada, and I suppose this is the official send-off. Foreign country, next stop, and all that. Want to go on over and introduce ourselves?"

Ben looked at his dusty coveralls. He shook his head. "There were thousands of us in the Army Air Service, Hank. Those fellows don't know if we're alive or dead. Let's just watch."

Shortly before one o'clock the deep, throaty roar of planes sounded in the east. Four De Havillands, bigger than the old Jenny, with four-hundred-horsepower Liberty motors, swept in perfect formation over the field, then circled three times. White faces could be seen peering over the cockpit, looking anxiously down to the ground.

"Maybe they didn't believe it when they were told this field used to be the city dump," Hank said to Ben.

"Quiet."

The first De Havilland came in, wings wide, wheels reaching for the grass-strewn runway. A flier jumped out hurriedly and glanced down at the thin tires. Almost at the same time, two other planes in the squadron bumped to a dusty halt before the spectators.

"That's Captain Streett," Ben said to Hank, "climbing out of Number One."

"Sure, and that's Ed Henriques, his mechanic—I used to pull duty with him regular! Let's get on over and ask him to lunch!"

Ben shook his head. "There are five hundred people waiting here to take those fellows to lunch. They're famous. We'd just be in the way—" He bit off his words, looking sharply at the fourth plane bumping and rolling to a landing. "He's in trouble!"

The last De Havilland screeched and skidded along the dirt, rising and falling with the irregular humps like a ship breasting heavy swells. Suddenly it came to a vicious halt, slewing to one side.

"Well, now," Hank said, starting toward the plane, "what that fellow needs is a good mechanic—me."

"Get back there, you." The big army sergeant glared at Hank. "We can fix our own planes without a couple of empty heads horning in."

Hank bristled.

"Come on, Hank," Ben counseled. "He's right. Let's get out of here."

"Ben," Hank pleaded, "can't we even listen to the speeches?"

Ben relented. The two edged through the crowd toward the five army officers and three sergeants who were lined up by the olive-green fuselage of the first plane. Ben's heart leaped when he recognized Captain Streett, Lieutenant Kirkpatrick and Lieutenant Crumrine. He started forward. At that moment a general stepped before the men and began reading a long speech.

"Epoch-making, blazing new trails, pioneers to the north, sturdy planes, brave fliers—" The words went on and on.

Hank swatted flies that were buzzing about. "All the talk in the world won't get that tail skid fixed. They better start hustling if they want to get off before dark."

Suddenly the speech ended, the general disappeared and the crowd began to thin. Ben, starting to walk toward the officers, was suddenly overcome with shyness and held back. In those few minutes

40

the five officers stepped into a car and were driven toward the town of Portal. Ben watched them drive off. "Shucks," he whispered to himself, "they wouldn't remember me anyhow." He walked over to the crippled plane and joined the men who were staring glumly at the broken tail skid.

"If they'll just listen to me," Hank said impatiently, "I'll have that thing fixed in a couple of hours." He approached the men and suggested a quick way to use available materials.

"Who ever heard of using an auto axle for a tail skid brace?" one of the army sergeants demanded belligerently.

Ben grinned. "Just you listen to this fellow, Sergeant, and you'll be all right. He found out a long time ago you don't need all the nuts and bolts to keep a plane flying."

All afternoon and early evening Hank and Ben worked with the three sergeants attached to the flight. When the tail skid was fixed, the army men shook hands solemnly with the two gypsy fliers. "We'd have been sitting here for days waiting for parts to be sent out from Chicago. You sure got this flight on the way to Alaska."

The next morning, after sleeping beneath the wings of their Jenny, Ben and Hank were on hand to see the men of the Black Wolf Squadron climb into their planes. Props were spun and four Liberty motors roared. One after the other the ships took to the air, turning north and crossing the border into Canada a short distance away.

"Here's our chance, Ben," Hank said excitedly. "Those planes have gone, but we've still got the crowd. How about a sales pitch?"

"Not today." Suddenly Ben felt dispirited. Those men in the four De Havillands were doing something for aviation. He was only a circus performer.

For weeks afterward he was restless while he traced the route of the Black Wolf Squadron on its flight north to Alaska. The De Havillands flew in rain and fog and storm. They smashed wings and undercarriages and blew tires while landing in wheat fields and clearings ripped from scrub-pine forests in northern Canada. They staggered and limped, but they continued to push northward for five tortuous weeks while a whole world watched. The De Havillands were likened to gallant wounded soldiers struggling through a wilderness to reach a sworn destination. But they made it. They flew to Fairbanks, then on to Nome on the Bering Sea. For the first time America realized that Alaska could be reached by air.

From that day on, Ben's eyes were fixed on the northland.

One afternoon, before a sell-out crowd, he lowered his plane above a speeding automobile, holding his course level a few feet above the car. Hank lowered himself from the wing, dangled until his feet touched the top of the car, then let go. Scores of times before, the transfer had been successful. This time Hank teetered on the car, clutched for support and fell to the ground. By the time Ben landed the airplane and taxied to a halt, the little stunt man had been carried to a hospital. Ben found him being readied for an operation on a shattered leg, grinning despite the pain.

"Well, this closes our bag of tricks," Ben said. "I'm so grateful you're still alive. I'm getting out."

Hank shook his head vigorously. "Not me, Ben. This is the excuse I've been waiting for."

"What do you mean?"

"I won't be able to do wing walking again— that's for sure. But I'm getting a promotion. I'm going to start flying these planes. Ben," he said excitedly, as the nurse started to wheel him down the corridor toward the operating room, "I've got my name picked out for the posters. 'Fearless Hank Robinson.' " He was silent a moment, then reared up from the cart, "No. It'll be 'Fearless Frank Robinson!' Watch my smoke!"

A few days later Ben took the Jenny up alone. At the take-off he rammed headlong into some telephone wires. The plane was utterly demolished, but Ben walked away unhurt.

He decided to go back to school, trying to pick up the loose ends of the law education he had started long before. Once it had been the University of Wisconsin that had attracted him by the excellent reputation of its law school; now it was Georgetown University of Washington, D.C. He went home to say good-by to his family and then left by train for Washington.

Letters from Hank Robinson followed him. Known as "Fearless Frank Robinson," he was thrilling the West Coast with daredevil feats never before witnessed. "I'm putting this airplane through the wringer every day in the week," Hank boasted in his letter, "and the crowd loves it. Why don't you forget school? Come on out with me and we'll fly as a team. Two planes, double the money! We'll be rich inside a year!"

Ben needed the money, but he avoided Hank's tempting offer. Despite the long hours of study demanded by his law course, he worked as a Congressional guard in the Capitol Building. There he met Dan Sutherland, a former miner and now Alaska's delegate to Congress. A mutual liking sprang up immediately between the two and Sutherland told Ben of the Gold Rush days, while Ben recounted anecdotes of his barnstorming with Hank Robinson.

One afternoon Dan Sutherland tossed a letter over to Ben. "They need a general-science teacher up at the Fairbanks High School. Know anybody who'd be interested in the job?"

Ben shook his head, smiling slightly. "If you

mean me, no. I'm quitting law school, that's true, but only because I'm going out to the West Coast and join Hank Robinson. I can't get flying out of my mind."

The next day he was sitting in the deep leather chair in the delegate's office. He was white-faced and trembling. He tried to keep his eyes on the big yellow map of Alaska hung on the wall behind the delegate's desk. The wide spaces seemed to swim, the names became a blur. Faintly and far away he could hear the barreling roar of an airplane skimming the waters of the Potomac River. He came to his feet when Dan Sutherland entered the office.

"You read the paper this morning, Mr. Sutherland?" he asked.

"Yes, I did, Ben. I'm sorry."

It was a small item with a San Francisco dateline:

This afternoon, while stunting at 2,000 feet, the plane piloted by Fearless Frank Robinson went out of control. First one wing ripped off, then the other. Plane and pilot plummeted into San Francisco Bay. Robinson was dead when hauled from the water.

Ben steadied himself on Sutherland's desk. "If that teaching job is still open," he said, "I'd like to go to Alaska."

CHAPTER 4

Delegate Dan Sutherland was called out of Washington unexpectedly, and without his help Ben discovered that traveling to Alaska was like embarking for a foreign land. No one in Washington was quite sure of the best way to get north. The only thing everyone seemed to agree on was that the trip must start by boat from Seattle.

All the way across the country Ben read books on Alaska that he had crammed into his traveling bag before leaving. The few people he met who had been there were survivors of the Gold Rush days more than twenty years before. Their recollections had dimmed, and most of them had been so caught up in their personal hardships and adventures that they had lost perspective on time and distance in the Far North.

"You better hurry, sonny," one whiskered old-timer told him in the club car of the speeding train. "That ocean up there, she freezes solid, and you just won't be able to get in or out of Alaska. You just get stuck—tight!" The old man held his two clenched fists before him and glowered at Ben.

46

"But sir," Ben protested, "I've just finished reading in John Muir's book that the ocean never freezes south of the Aleutian Islands! Juneau and Valdez and Seward are ice-free the year round."

"They are?" The old-timer grunted and looked at Ben suspiciously. "Well, come to think of it, guess maybe they are. I was thinking of Nome, up there in the Bering Sea. Say, sonny, did I tell you about the time I landed on the beach at Nome, and smallpox was killing people like they were fleas? You see, it was like this—"

"Excuse me, I've got to look after my baggage. We're coming into Seattle."

The old-timer shook his head in disappointment. "Just dying right and left of us, that's what they were."

He was still mumbling when Ben left the club car and went forward to pick up his baggage.

Ben was worried. According to the wire he had received from Mr. Keller, Superintendent of the Fairbanks High School, opening ceremonies were scheduled for September 18th. That was only a week away.

At the steamship office in Seattle, the clerk, a thin wisp of a man speaking in a vague, dreamy manner, assured him that after nearly seven years of construction, the Alaska Railroad was accepting passengers for Fairbanks in the interior.

"Of course," the little man said cautiously, "if

you want to be sure, you can get off the steamship in Valdez and take the stage up over the Richardson Trail." He nodded his head eagerly. "Fine scenery."

"You made the trip?" Ben asked him.

The clerk shook his head dolefully. He lifted a dusty tourist circular. "Nope. Just been reading about it. In here." He started to read again, slowly, his finger following each word, his lips forming the syllables.

Ben shook his head. He picked up his ticket and his bag and went aboard the steamer *Northwestern*. When the blaring whistle finally sounded and the ship moved out into Elliott Bay, it seemed to give an added shake to its propeller, as though anxious to be gone north.

There were few passengers aboard and Ben was lonely. He stood at the rail as the little vessel carefully picked a pathway through the close-pressing islands. Towering mountains, densely covered with spruce, loomed over the ship, almost crushing it. At times the waterway narrowed to a space scarcely a hundred yards wide. Ben looked up to the men who paced the bridge. He could hear the quiet words spoken. He could feel the slight change in course as the *Northwestern* responded to the gentle pressure on the wheel. Then the current took hold of the vessel and hurled it headlong through a narrow opening between two islands.

For almost a thousand miles the ship took the same determined course through the Inside Passage, twisting and turning, avoiding treacherous rocks that were betrayed by the battered hulks of wrecked ships. The rain fell gently, and there was a growing chill in the air. The mountains looming on either side were snow-capped.

"Shore is pretty, ain't it, son?"

A little man, slightly stooped, unclenched a pipe from his teeth and pointed jerkily to the close-hemming mountains.

"What's that? I'm sorry," Ben apologized. "I just wasn't listening."

"I said them thar mountains shore is pretty, ain't they?"

"Yes, they are. Lot different from the scenery in North Dakota."

"North Dakota? You're a long way from home, mister. You going prospecting?" The question was asked cautiously.

"No. I'm going to be teaching up at the Fairbanks High School."

"Oh!" The little man blew a shower of sparks from his pipe. "Ain't never—I mean, I've never met a man schoolteacher before. Ones I knew in Nome was ladies."

Ben flushed and started to move away. The little man came after him.

"Now, now, don't go off mad, young fellow. I

heard tell a man schoolteacher took up prize fighting, and you know what, he became champeen of the world! Mark my words. Maybe you'll become a prize fighter—or something." His voice trailed off.

Ben looked upward at the mountains hemming in the ship on every side. Without realizing it, he said, "I just want to fly!"

The little man looked at him oddly, shaking his head. "I guess I just don't hear right any more. Could've sworn you said something about flying."

Ben started to reply, then shook his head. What was the use? He'd never fly again. He'd never again feel the slight tremble of a stick in the palm of his hand, never catch the cool touch of the wind on his cheek, never know the thrill of taking a fine ship headlong down an airstrip, lifting it into the air, swelling with the freedom offered only in the clouds. "I'm going inland from Seward," he said. "I understand I can catch a train there."

"Hear tell the same thing, and I'm sure going to take advantage of it. I been walking over Alaska so much, stumbling over muskeg and getting soaked in rivers—if I got a chance to sit right comfortable in a train and have someone take me, I'm going." He thrust out his gnarled hand. "My name's MacKenzie, son. Jasper Jay MacKenzie. Maybe you'll let me tag along and tell you a few things about the territory—even if you are a schoolteacher."

"Mine's Ben Eielson. And I'd be happy to have you tell me anything about the territory."

"Well, first thing you want to learn is—don't miss a chance to eat. That's the first call for dinner. Come along and let's see what we're getting for our passage money."

Jasper MacKenzie was one of the few men who had come north to Alaska in the Gold Rush days of '98 and '99—and stayed with the country. From Dawson he had drifted down the Yukon to Nome. When the gold had disappeared from the beaches, the little man had fought his way back up river, battling the current and the swarms of mosquitoes, following the bending pathway of the Yukon River as it looped across the heartland of Alaska. He had been on the heels of Felix Pedro when that mustachioed gentleman had made the first strike near Fairbanks. He had made the trek over the Valdez Glacier in search of gold and hurried after the hidden mountains of copper. For more than twenty years he had moved over the face of Alaska, seeing men all about him alternately gaining wealth and suffering poverty. He had pushed through the years never quite finding riches.

"I'm telling you, Ben," Jasper continued mournfully while he studied the baked potato on his plate, "things have changed. Used to be this country was on fire with excitement." He adjusted his false teeth and took a huge bite of the potato. "Now there's nothing. Like the land was asleep."

The motion of the *Northwestern* as it turned west and started across the heaving Gulf of Alaska made Ben uneasy. He watched Jasper chewing vigorously on the potato. "What do you mean?"

"Just like that story we used to read when we were kids. 'Sleeping Beauty.' The gal that got put to sleep by some witch and just kept snoozin' away until a prince came by and bussed her on the lips —if you remember the story."

"I remember."

Jasper nodded vigorously and took a tremendous mouthful of potato. "That's what we need up in this country," he said after several vigorous gulps. "We need a hero. You know what I mean?"

Ben shook his head. "No, I don't." He looked uneasily at the food on his plate. "Guess I don't feel well. I'm going to turn in."

"Just go right ahead, Ben," Jasper MacKenzie said, reaching over for Ben's plate. "I'll be waiting for you when you wake up." At that moment the ship gave a violent pitch and yaw. Jasper's hand stopped in mid-air. His face twisted and he looked oddly from the food to the floor. "On second thought," he said weakly, "maybe I'll turn in and take a nap myself." He pushed back his chair, clutched his hands to his stomach and suddenly bolted from the dining room.

When the *Northwestern* entered Prince William Sound after crossing the Gulf of Alaska, Ben remained in his stateroom. He admitted to himself ruefully that he did not want to come to Alaska, that he had turned north only because he was running away from thoughts of Hank Robinson and his friend's tragic death. He admitted that he was drawn to teaching, not for the true motives of trying to help younger people attain a finer knowledge of the world, but as an escape.

He shook himself. "Come out of it, Eielson," he said aloud. "You've been playing the baby too long. You're here in Alaska. You're going to teach. And you're going to do the very best job you know how."

He reached for his hat and went out and stood on the deck. On every side were vistas of restless, snow-tipped monuments in a jumble of majestic beauty, the harsh mountains reflected in the soft green waters of the sound. There were glaciers to be seen at every hand, and in the water small icebergs floated quietly out to sea.

When the ship entered the twenty-mile stretch of smooth water called Resurrection Bay, sailing quietly past two grim islands and slipping cautiously past a jagged tooth of bare rock squarely in the middle of the channel, Jasper MacKenzie, his whiskered face an ashen white, came to stand at Ben's side. "Man, oh, man," he said, "all of a sudden I didn't care if this ship sank. Never been so upset in my life. Look ahead there, Ben. You can just see the pier. Right beyond must be them train cars that's going to ride us in comfort to the richest gold strike Alaska ever knew. How times has changed!"

Carl Ben Eielson's arrival in Alaska was an inauspicious one. It was raining. Hard driving gusts were sweeping over the mountains that hemmed in Resurrection Bay, and thudding down with almost perceptible noise into the placid water of the land-locked harbor. The ominous clouds sagged down heavily, forming a wavering line of gray-white that obscured the mountaintops. By the time Ben had walked down the gangplank and along the dock to the train that waited not too far distant, he was soaked.

Jasper MacKenzie waved grandly to the mountains almost obscured by the clouds. "What do you think?"

"Wet."

"What?"

"I think it's wet."

"Oh."

When they sat together on the hard green cushions of the train, Jasper peered anxiously at Ben. "You're shivering."

"Sure thing. I'll probably get pneumonia."

"Ah, pshaw, Ben! Big, strong fellow like you—

you won't even get the sniffles! Why, man, I've gone up and down this country—wet, dry, cold, hot, sweaty and shivering—and I ain't never got so much as a sneeze. Brace up." He dug into his pocket. "Have a chaw of tobacco."

"No, thanks."

Jasper sank back, lifted his boots and rested them grandly on the seat before him.

"This is the life," he said.

Ben kept staring through the rain-smeared window as the train churned along the tracks. There were endless seas of birch on either side, then the milky white and pale green waters of Lake Kenai. The train inched cautiously over high wooden trestles that spanned immense canyons, then twisted and turned and climbed over itself as it reached higher and higher on the grade. When they went past a little clearing, he could see settlers coming and staring at the creaking train. Ben looked up at the smooth-sided, white-peaked mountains that waited calmly on either side, moving slightly in misty clouds. Vast meadows of grass rolled upward along the sides of the mountains.

"Rain's stopping," Jasper MacKenzie said softly.

The clouds began to fade away.

Ben began to respond to the insistent magnetism of the land. Everything was so vast, so overpowering. The mountains were incredibly big, incredibly close, and there seemed to be no end to them.

"Bear out there," Jasper said, pointing. "Big brown bear. And the whole peninsula is so chock full of moose you could fall over them."

Through Moose Pass the train labored, then along the beaver dams of Trail Creek. It strained mightily and made the summit at Grandview, picking up speed as though glad the worst of the struggle was over. It inched past Bartlett Glacier and Spencer Glacier, hung to the side of rivers and climbed the stony sides of mountains. The land was so close that Ben felt he was being pinned beneath the lofty giants.

Glory, he thought, I'd hate to walk over them. He looked closer at the snow-covered peaks and whispered, "I'd love to fly over them. I'd love to take a Jenny and fly past those peaks. I'd brush a wing tip down and trace a line in the snow like Hank Robinson used to do on the beaches in California. Someday someone will bring a plane over those mountains—I hope I'm the one to do it."

The train picked up speed. Suddenly the whistle of the steam engine ahead started tooting wildly.

Jasper MacKenzie leaped to his feet, pulled up the window and thrust his head far out. "By golly," he yelled over his shoulder, "I heard tell of it, but I never believed it. Get your head out here, Ben, and take a look!"

Ben leaned far out into the wind, blinking at the shower of cinders that struck him in the face.

Shielding his eyes, he was able to look ahead as the train bent to a curve. Galloping heavily down the track was an enormous moose, antlers twisting from side to side as it looked backward over its broad shoulders.

"Them there silly animals like to run down the track," Jasper yelled into Ben's ear. "When he gets tired of running—watch out!"

Suddenly the moose stopped. It spun about, lowered its head, pawed at the ties and bellowed in rage at the onrushing train. Brakes screeched, whistles tooted, but the momentum carried the train forward. There was a thudding contact. The train lurched, buckled to one side, then bumped heavily to a halt.

Jasper pulled at Ben, dragging him back inside. "Dang near lost you, too. Let's get up front and see who lost the battle."

They ran the length of the train to the engine. The big bull moose was sprawled in death, its six-foot antlers tangled in the cowcatcher in front of the chunky locomotive. The conductor was staring morosely at the huge carcass. "Well," he said, "first car is derailed." He bent down and seized a leg. "Come on. Give a hand here and drag him to one side." He grunted heavily. "Three quarters of a ton if he's an ounce. The orphanage'll be eating moose steaks for the next month."

Ben helped drag the big animal aside. Then he

and Jasper worked with the train crew while heavy jacks were placed under the trucks of the first car, and the wheels were shoved back on the rails.

Jasper MacKenzie wiped his brow. "It still beats walking. Let's get aboard and rest up. I have only enough strength for one moose at a time."

After they were seated, a rough hand reached out and yanked Jasper's boots to the floor. "Get those boots off that seat, mister. This is a passenger train, not a cattle car."

"Why, you—" Jasper leaped to his feet, bristling.

The big, burly conductor lowered his head and stared him in the eye. "Government property, mister. You got any complaints, report 'em to the Secretary of the Interior."

"I got lots of complaints." Jasper cocked his fist and advanced on the conductor.

Ben reached out and took the little man by the shoulder, hauling him back to the seat.

"Calm down. The conductor's right. We've got to get to Fairbanks, and we'll never be able to fight our way up there."

"Fairbanks?" The conductor turned his head. "This train only goes to Anchorage. Line isn't finished into Fairbanks—not by a long sight."

Ben leaped to his feet. "Doesn't go to Fairbanks? I was told down in Seattle—"

"Don't care what they told you in Seattle, young

fellow. The Alaska Railroad isn't finished—you'll get off the train in Anchorage—and that's that. Long way up to Fairbanks. Three hundred and seventy miles, maybe. Tough walking."

CHAPTER 5

Ben paced back and forth, not believing the conductor's words. "No rail service into Fairbanks? I'll have to get back to Seward, take a boat over to Valdez and the stage overland from there! I'll be at least a week late for the opening of school."

"That's your worry, mister," the conductor told him.

"I could fly up to Fairbanks in less than three hours," Ben answered bitterly.

"Calm down, now, Ben," Jasper counseled. "We ain't licked yet. I got friends in Anchorage. Just you settle back and enjoy the scenery. I'll get you up to Fairbanks if I have to carry you up on my back."

Ben shook his head. "When we get to Anchorage I'll send a wire to Mr. Keller and tell him I expect to be late. Fine start this is." He looked up suddenly. "Maybe I won't even be able to send a telegram." He walked hastily after the retreating conductor. "Is there telegraph service between Anchorage and Fairbanks?"

"Of course." He hesitated a moment. "Sorry to be so grumpy, young fellow, but them moose always get me upset. Seems I spend half my time on this railroad chasing animals off the track."

Ben was so dispirited that he scarcely realized what the conductor was saying. The train crept around the vast mud flats of Turnagain Arm. Far to the left he could see a long, rectangular-shaped mountain thrust upward from the horizon. Jasper stirred at his side, peered with one eye through the window and said, "Mount Susitna. The Sleeping Lady, we call her. We should be pulling into Anchorage any minute."

The train ground to a halt and the two swung off. Ben walked toward the station. Jasper MacKenzie grasped his arm. "I'm telling you, Ben. I got friends!"

Ben shook his head. "Sorry, Jasper. I've got to get up to Fairbanks. I can't take any more chances."

He went inside the station and purchased a ticket on the southbound train leaving that night. "Can I check my bag in the station?"

"Sure thing, fellow."

He walked up the steep hill leading to the plateau where the town of Anchorage was laid out along unpaved streets. Wooden store fronts faced each other across the wide expanse. Sounds of hammering filled the air. Large signs of real-estate brokers announcing the sale of town lots were thick on all sides.

He tried walking faster, his long strides carrying him easily over the mud puddles left from the recent rain. He walked past the crowded camp of the itinerant railroad workers, and kept going farther and farther beyond the town on the rough, rutted road. There were fine clearings in the immense stands of birch, and his airman's eye assessed them, visualizing the possibility of small airfields. "Why couldn't they have some planes up here?" he asked himself.

The western skies began to darken. Black storm clouds came over the prone form of Mount Susitna. Ben turned and hurried toward Anchorage. He heard the faint blaring whistle of trains on the flats below.

Far off on Knik Arm he could see small salmon trollers edging closer to shore. An immense raft of spruce logs was being floated toward the mud flats. The smooth waters of Knik Arm began to ruffle like the feathers of a bird as the wind took hold and played upon it.

Ben hurried down the wooden sidewalks. He was

61

hungry and looked forward to a fine meal before getting on the train for the backward run down to Seward that night.

"Hey, Ben! Ben!"

Spinning about, he saw Jasper MacKenzie waving at him from across the street.

"Ben! I found us a way. We're heading for Fairbanks. Wait up, Ben!"

The little man started across the muddy street.

"Watch it, Jasper, watch that dray!"

Down the street, lurching and pulling, came an enormous dray loaded with cut lumber. It swerved from side to side in trying to avoid the rain puddles.

"Watch it, Jasper!" Ben yelled, but the little man, apparently not seeing the onrushing dray, ran straight into the path of the big horses. There was a short cry, then Jasper MacKenzie was engulfed in a swirl of motion. The driver pulled hard on the reins; the horses reared, feet stomping furiously. Ben heard the familiar querulous voice screaming, "Well, dad blast it, mister, if I couldn't drive a team of horses better'n that I'd get me a Mack truck!"

Jasper crawled out from under the wagon, shaking himself like a little terrier dog, glowering at the white-faced driver.

"You hurt? You want me to drive you to—" the driver asked.

"Get going, you, or I'll show you who's hurt!" Jasper brandished his clenched fist and the driver spoke urgently to the horses.

Ben ran across and put his arm about the old man's shoulder.

"Jasper," he said, "I thought I'd seen the last of you."

"Pshaw," the little man replied, shaking the mud from his clothes, "isn't a horse in the whole territory of Alaska could stomp a hole in my head. I mind the time once I was leading a pack train across the West Fork of the Kuskokwim, and this horse he took a notion to bite a hunk of my leg off. Well, you know, I just wrestled around with that animal, holding his head under water so long he called quits. Best danged horse I ever owned after that." He patted his cheek reflectively, then suddenly turned about. "What I started to say, Ben, when them danged army mules tromped me—I got us a way to get to Fairbanks, quick! I tell you, I got friends. I ain't been sitting around this country for twenty-two years playing solitaire—not by a long sight, I ain't."

"I can't wait," Ben argued. "I can't take any more chances, Jasper. I sent a wire to Mr. Keller saying I'd be a week late. If I just follow out the plan I made, everything will be fine."

"You're due in Fairbanks on the 18th—four days from now. You're not going to make it backtrack-

63

ing like a bull moose sniffing its own trail. Fairbanks is up that way, Ben," Jasper said dramatically, pointing almost due north, "and you're heading south again to salt water. Don't make sense."

"Tell me your plan."

"Work trains are leaving Anchorage every day for the end-of-construction up at Nenana. We go down to the yards tomorrow morning at sunup, skedaddle aboard—and away we go!"

"What happens when we get to Nenana?" Ben asked doubtfully. "That's still fifty, sixty miles from Fairbanks. What do we do then—walk?"

Jasper lifted his shoulders. "I could do that on my hands. Are you coming, Ben?"

The big blond youth hesitated. Suddenly he thrust out his hand. "Why not? Come on. I'll treat you to the best dinner in town!"

Sleeping space in the boom town of Anchorage was at a premium. Ben and Jasper spent that night in bunks around the boiler room of a small hotel just off Fourth Avenue. It seemed to Ben he had just fallen asleep when Jasper was shaking him and whispering urgently, "Got to get moving, Ben. That work train isn't going to wait for us."

They dressed quietly, for the boiler room was jammed with sleeping men. Jasper looked about in the darkness. "Sounds like they was strangling," he sniffed. "Never heard such awful snoring in my life."

Out on the streets, thin crusts of night frost were still on the rain puddles. Ben pulled his coat tighter about him. "I'll feel better after I get some breakfast."

"No time for eating, Ben," Jasper said hurriedly. "We'll just have to get aboard and hope for the best."

They hurried down the steep hill to the rail yards, walking past long rows of empty flatcars. The light was coming stronger as the sun began to glint on the white top of Mount Susitna. They came to a row of cars stacked high with railroad ties, telegraph poles, bridge steel and bulky rolls of copper wiring.

"Up you go, Ben," Jasper whispered. "Climb up and snuggle down among those ties."

"Wait a minute," Ben protested. "We don't have to sneak aboard, do we? I've got money to pay—"

"Now, now, don't get upset. Just throw your leg up that ladder—and don't make so dang much noise!"

Ben threw his bag aboard a flatcar and climbed upward. He felt his way over an uneven stack of ties, found an opening and dropped out of sight on the rough floor of the railroad car. Jasper Mac-Kenzie tumbled in after him. When Ben started to speak, Jasper held his finger to his lips. "Later, Ben," he hissed. "Later."

In a few minutes Ben could hear the sound of

heavy footsteps crunching in the night-frozen gravel alongside the tracks. Far away there was a faint call, then the engine hooted mournfully in response. There was a terrific lurch, a grinding movement and suddenly the train was in motion. Ben felt the ties at the back of his head. When he drew back his hand it was moist.

"Ben, you're bleeding!" Jasper looked at the hand with concern.

"No such luck. That's creosote. This Pullman car you've ordered is loaded with freshly creosoted ties, that's all. What a sight we'll be when we get out of here!"

Jasper clucked deprecatingly. Then he sighed and snuggled his thin shoulders back against the ties. "Still beats walking, that's all I got to say."

The sun came higher and higher and a warm golden glow spread over the stacked ties on the railroad car as the train picked up speed and headed for the Matanuska Valley. The never-ending stands of birch were on either side, while beyond were the towering snow-clad mountains that Ben had already accepted as the trademark of Alaska. He listened to the steady clack-clack of the wheels racing over the steel rails, each measured sound bringing them closer and closer to Fairbanks. Throw these clothes away, a good bath, a big meal—and I'll be able to forget this ride, he thought to himself.

All day they remained on the wooden car, looking out at the land flowing behind—dark green grass fading into brown, the trees bared already before the coming winter, as the train snaked a course through the Susitna Valley, inching higher and higher through the range of mountains that blocked off the tundra of the interior from the flat expanse of the sea. Ben's hunger was gargantuan. He kept looking at the mountains, floating close by on the horizon, and his mind transformed them into tremendous sandwiches. As he watched the waters of the Susitna River racing by, he envisioned them as an endless stream of boiling hot coffee. He saw the dozens of glaciers dropping down from the mountain valleys as mammoth dishes of ice cream just beyond reach. He was jolted out of his reverie as Jasper nudged him.

"Keep looking sharp there to the west, and you'll get yourself a look at McKinley."

"Mount McKinley?"

"What else? Most days it's so hidden in clouds you can't see a thing. But I got a hunch today will be different."

Ben twisted to one side, looking toward the thick cluster of mountains that faded abruptly one into the other as though merged into a family of giants. But gradually, as the train churned forward, he could make out one colossus looming above the others. His eyes lifted above the thin veil of clouds, past the glaciers and the vast snow fields, and finally rested on the feathery crest of Mount McKinley, highest in the North American continent. "Golly," he whispered. "Hate to be flying close to that fellow on a dark night."

"Just thank your lucky stars you don't have to climb over it to get some place," Jasper grunted. "When I come up to Skagway in '98, trying to get into Dawson, we were shinnying up the face of Chilkoot Pass. Sometimes it seemed twice as high and twice as hard to get over as that there mountain." He looked about. "Man, I got to get something to eat fast before my stomach takes a permanent vacation."

He sniffed cautiously, his mustache leaping upward with each movement of his nostrils. "Nearest thing to a hot turkey sandwich I ever did smell." He began to move his head from side to side.

Ben smiled. Jasper reminded him of an old dog that he had owned as a boy in North Dakota. "Watch you don't fall off, Jasper."

MacKenzie was on his hands and knees peering over the side of the flatcar. "By golly, Ben," he called over his shoulder, "we're on fire! That danged wheel is smoking like a burned potato!"

Even as he spoke, the train lurched heavily as the brakes were applied. The forward motion eased, then stopped entirely. From the rear of the train a brakeman came running, a tin pail in his

hand, followed by the conductor, clad in blue over-
alls and a sweater. They looked up at Ben and
Jasper, blinked in astonishment, then turned their
attention to the wheel.

"Hotbox," the conductor snorted. "Let's cool it
off fast."

The brakeman tumbled down a small embankment to the creek paralleling the tracks. He swung
his pail and broke the skim ice, then dipped into
the water. As he struggled up the embankment,
Ben, who had leaped down from the car, helped
him over the edge. The water was thrown on the
steaming axle, hissing and sputtering. Three times
the brakeman clambered down for water. Then he
tossed the pail aside. "If I go down there once
more, I won't be able to come back."

Ben seized the pail and made a fourth trip.

"That'll do, son," the conductor said. He had the
lid of the waste box open and was jabbing vigorously with a stick trying to remove the smoking
remnants of waste. The wisps of cotton, saturated
with grease, came out in charred hunks. "Joe," he
called to the brakeman, "get the jacks under the
axle."

The brakeman shook his head. He was still
breathing heavily. "Can't. I'm all in."

"I'll get them," Ben volunteered.

"Back in the caboose, in the locker to the right.
Careful you don't drop 'em on your toes."

Ben struggled back with the heavy jacks. With Jasper's assistance, he shoved them under the axle and started pumping vigorously, trying to lift the axle so that new waste could be crammed into the bearing box. But the more he pumped, the less his efforts prevailed.

"Hold it, son, you're just digging a hole down to China. Take the jack out and put some big shims under it. You're forcing the ties deeper into this wet ground."

Once more they tried, this time with the weight of the big jack on a piece of four-by-six spread across several ties. The axle lifted. The conductor rammed in new waste, poured oil copiously over the packing and finally grunted in satisfaction.

"That'll do it," he said. He looked at Ben and Jasper. "Getting cold out here. You two better come back in the caboose and explain how come you're hitching rides on government property."

In the caboose Ben and Jasper wolfed down the sandwiches the conductor provided. They sat close to the roaring oil stove, for the air had grown intensely cold as night closed in. The train twisted through Nenana Canyon, ducked through several tunnels, then clanked and rattled while it bored through the night, heading for the dim, winking lights that marked the small town of Nenana.

"Come with me," the conductor said. "I'll fix it

for you to sleep in the camp with the bridge workers, and get you a ride into Fairbanks, too."

The next morning, in the chill light of predawn,
Ben stood on a work train looking back at the
piers of a steel bridge which, when completed,
would be the last link in the railroad piercing the
heart of Alaska.

In a few hours he would be in Fairbanks. He
had kept his word to arrive in time for the opening
of the high school.

CHAPTER 6

"Good-by, Jasper."

Ben held out his hand to the little man who stood
expertly in the small boat bobbing on the swift waters of the Chena Slough. Above them was the
crisscross steelwork of a narrow bridge. Beyond
were the low wooden buildings sheltering the fifteen hundred men, women and children who called
Fairbanks home.

"You sure you won't change your mind, Ben?"

"I've given my word, Jasper. The school board
would never be able to get a replacement."

Jasper nodded as he sat down and grasped the oars. "Guess I knew all the time you wouldn't." He looked up at Ben hopefully. "Maybe next summer when school's out, eh?"

"Maybe. Write to me. I'll find you." He let go of the restraining tether that held the small boat. Almost immediately the current took hold of the craft and swept it into midstream. The little man held his hand aloft in farewell. Then the current swept him and the boat out of sight.

Ben listened to the racing water. He knew that Jasper would follow the slough down to the Tanana River, then ride with the current into the wide Yukon, using the rivers as a highway across the face of Alaska. With all his heart he wanted to share the adventures that were awaiting Jasper on his lonely prospecting trip, yet never for a moment did he contemplate breaking his word to the school board.

He left the river, scrambling up the bank through the birch trees, and walked back over the bridge toward the town. In that early September morning Fairbanks was still asleep. Ben passed an old man puttering around outside a cabin, a tiny building six feet wide and ten feet long, surrounded by a row of five-gallon oilcans set six inches away from the wall. The space between the cans and the cabin was filled with sawdust, protection against the long fingers of sub-zero weather that would come with the onrushing winter. Workmen were preparing big wooden boxes to place about the fireplugs for insulation against the coming cold. In an open excavation Ben could see the steam pipes from the Northern Commercial Company snuggled close to the water pipes in order to keep the latter from freezing in the permanently frozen soil just beneath the surface.

Along Cushman Street was a hodgepodge of business buildings, dark and quiet in this early-morning hour. Turning to the right, he walked on wooden sidewalks lining dirt streets. The homes that he passed were comfortable-looking, with a bit of grass-covered ground about each, all of them protected from the cold by a double thickness of sawdust and dirt crammed about the foundations. From some of the chimneys sparks leaped upward, wavering through the air to land on the corrugated iron roofs.

There was the smell of wood smoke in the air, and a restful quiet in the calm atmosphere that was entirely devoid of sound.

Ben kicked at the frost that had formed during the night. It was going to be a long winter, and he dreaded the dark days of loneliness ahead. Far in the distance, by a bend in the slough, he heard a chorus of howls from the pound where monster sled dogs were boarded until the coming of snow.

He stopped before a boxy, two-story wooden

building marked FAIRBANKS SCHOOL. Above the roof was a square belfry. He tried the door and it was unlocked. He went in, walked the silent halls and sat down at a desk in a classroom. The only sound was that of steam crackling in the radiators.

In the strange, eerie quiet that marked the beginning of his teaching career, he thought of Hank Robinson, and tears came to his eyes.

"Get 'im talking about airplanes."

Ben heard the whisper as he turned from the blackboard. He tried to stop the grin that formed on his lips. In the three months that had passed since he had joined the high-school teaching staff which was composed of himself, Mr. Keller, Esther Smith and Hannah Sponheim, the forty-eight high-school students had seized every opportunity to distract him with questions about flying. And, he admitted to himself, they had succeeded.

"Mr. Eielson, if you had an airplane here in Fairbanks and wanted to fly to Seattle, how would you go about it?"

Ben sat on the desk, holding his right knee in his hand while he rocked slightly back and forth. Outside, the darkened clouds seemed to rest heavily on the wooden buildings of Fairbanks. There was a stillness in the air that told of the low temperatures to be expected with the night.

"Well," he replied, "first thing I'd do would be to take a map and draw a line between the two cities. Let's see—must be about eleven, twelve hundred miles. High mountains, no landing fields, no fuel waiting—any number of reasons why I'd have to change course from a straight line." He smiled ruefully, remembering his troubles with navigation. "If I had a fine wide river to follow, like the Yukon or the Tanana, guess I'd follow that even if it did take me a long way out of course. Or a railroad—that's best of all."

"No railroads to guide you between here and Seattle," a voice said from the rear row.

"That's true. Nothing but the White Pass and the Yukon, and that only stretches a hundred and ten miles—the wrong way. No," Ben concluded, "flying up in this country won't be easy. A pilot could get lost easier here than anywhere else."

"Maybe it's so hard nobody will ever want to fly up here."

Ben shook his head. "I'm ready. I'll fly the minute I get my hands on a plane," he said earnestly. "Somebody's got to start. And it's going to be done soon, I know." He spun about on the desk. "That's all. See you tomorrow."

After class a young boy came to Ben's desk. "Mr. Eielson, my dad wants to know if he can come see you."

"You mean, here at school? There's nothing

wrong with your work, Tad. Your marks are excellent."

"No, it's not that. My dad and some men, they've been asking me questions about you and airplanes—and anyhow, they got an idea, and they want to come see you."

"Any time. You know I'm living at the Alaska Hotel?"

"Yes. Can I tell Dad you'll see him tonight?"

"You sure can."

When he was alone, Ben walked to the schoolroom window and looked out at Fairbanks. The temperature was plummeting, preparing for the usual mid-January siege of bitter cold. The schoolchildren, bundled against the weather, walked hurriedly toward their homes, not bothering for the usual games about the red schoolhouse. He caught a glimpse of the thermometer. It was thirty degrees below zero. If the temperature continued to drop, school might be closed on the following day.

He closed his desk, put on his overcoat and fur hat and walked down the steps. The cold air came sharply into his lungs, biting almost as though it were a liquid. He remembered the intensely cold days of his youth in North Dakota. There, too, the temperatures had plummeted, but here in Fairbanks, the mercury, once down, stayed submerged. Three weeks had gone by with the temperature sagging far down to fifty and sixty degrees below zero.

The few automobiles on the streets moved slowly, as though the drivers were afraid the cold menaced the contraptions of wood and steel that they guided.

The townsfolk of Fairbanks had learned to live with the deadly temperatures, yet always with an air of caution.

When Ben returned to his hotel, there was a letter waiting for him from Jasper MacKenzie.

"Ben," he wrote, "I've got hold of a good-looking claim. Just picking away, now, trying to sink a shaft down through the sand, but from what I've been able to see, she looks good. Any chance you can shake loose from schoolteaching? Get yourself a team of dogs, and you'll be down here in no time— Sure would like to see you."

Ben looked at the map he had hung on the wall. McGrath was only three hundred miles away. Yet it had taken the letter nearly three weeks to reach him. What if he could load a plane with mail and fly into every corner of Alaska?

That night, in answer to a knock on his hotel-room door, Ben greeted a serious-looking businessman who was wrapped in an enormous fur coat.

"I'm Tad Hopkins' father, Professor Eielson." He sat down ponderously on a frail chair. "There's a group of businessmen who are convinced that what this country needs is a good airplane and a good pilot to fly it. Frankly, we don't know where to start—except by talking to someone who knows airplanes—what they can do and what they can't do. That's why I'm here to invite you to meet with my friends down at the newspaper office. Can you come?"

As they walked down the street in the bitter, silent cold and turned into the offices of the *News-Miner*, the daily paper, Ben felt a mounting excitement. His heart was beating quickly. Something was to come of this meeting, he was sure. He was introduced to Wrong Font Thompson, the editor of the publication, and Dick Wood, the town banker. Wood smiled apologetically while he shook Ben's hand. "You've got to excuse us, Professor, acting as though we were a bunch of conspirators. But to tell the truth, there are still a lot of people who think anyone interested in airplanes is either half crazy or completely crazy! Tell us about yourself. Where did you learn to fly?"

Briefly Ben sketched his army training, his days of gypsy flying, barnstorming about the Middle West. He said nothing about Hank Robinson and his tragic death. He didn't want to dampen the enthusiasm of the men who sat before him.

The trio nodded in agreement as Ben finished.

"Let me ask, Professor—or should I call you Ben?—from what you've seen of the country in the few months you've been here, do you think it feasible to operate an airplane in Alaska, not from a joy-riding standpoint, but from a hard, practical business point of view? To put it bluntly, could a businessman expect a reasonable profit out of the venture?"

Ben studied his big hands, picking his words carefully. "As far as winter flying is concerned—I don't know. Even the United States Army doesn't know very much about flying in cold weather. It's something we'd have to experiment with, because there's a thousand questions we would want answered. Nobody knows just how an airplane motor would act in temperatures like this. Nobody's sure what happens to the oil or the grease, even to the fuel. And no one could predict what would happen to a pilot who would be forced down on the tundra in sixty-below-zero weather."

He sensed the gloom coming over his listeners and went on hastily. "But in the spring and summer, I'm positive you could make an airplane pay for itself in a month's time! Look," he said convincingly, "I just received this letter today from a friend of mine down in McGrath. Took three weeks to reach me—and McGrath is less than three hundred miles away by air. Do you realize, gentlemen, if I had two refueling stations for a De Havilland plane, I could fly down to McGrath in less than three hours?"

Wrong Font Thompson fashioned a paper airplane and let it sail across the narrow office building. "That means, with a good plane, a good pilot and refueling stations, you could fly almost anywhere in Alaska in less than a day?"

"Exactly."

Thompson rose from his chair and strode nervously about the office. "I tell you, Dick," he said, addressing his remarks to the banker, "this is what we've been waiting for. For years I've been saying over and over in my column in the paper that it's lack of transportation that's holding back Alaska. Man, we can't get anywhere! In the winter we've got to rely on dog teams. In the summer, we've got to stick to the rivers. Juneau, the capital city, is only six hundred miles away—yet getting down there from Fairbanks is a major trip—like crossing the United States by covered wagon seventy-five years ago. Look at Nome," he said, banging his fist against a wall map. "Frozen tighter'n a nut from November to May. Takes a brave man to come overland by dog team during the winter. But with airplanes, there's no reason why we couldn't have daily service between Nome and Fairbanks! Service anywhere. With airplanes we can open up this country like a new book!"

Dick Wood shook his head. "Don't forget the railroad," he said cautiously. "It'll be finished next summer and we'll have two-day service down to Seward on the coast."

"Fine, fine, fine," Thompson said energetically, "the railroad's fine—but it isn't enough."

Ben thought of his own trip over the railroad a few months ago.

"What's more," Thompson continued, "we've waited nine years for the railroad to come, one single, solitary line four hundred and seventy miles long—if we wait for more railroads to open up Alaska we'll see two hundred years go by before we have lines comparable to those they have in the States."

"I was thinking," Ben said . . .

"No, Dick," Thompson continued, so excited that he did not notice Ben's interruption, "the railroad is good, but it's not the answer. We've been watching this territory for twenty-five years. We've seen the steamship come up and land our people on the coast; then we've seen them struggle over the Richardson Trail and along the river and over the dog trails trying to get inland. We've seen the flow of goods come almost to a complete stop every winter because it costs so dang much to get anything up here by sled. The whole country has been stagnating because people can't get around quickly—and I'm telling you, the airplane, and this young fellow to fly it, is the answer."

"I was thinking," Ben tried again mildly.

But once again he was ignored in the excitement of the meeting. Dick Wood shook his head stubbornly and started to speak. Ben shrugged his shoulders and sank back into the chair. They would just have to talk it out.

"Two, three years ago," Wood said sharply, "when those army planes flew up from Canada and went on to Nome and back to the States—you didn't see them setting any speed records, did you? And they had the entire United States helping them—landing fields, gasoline, rescue parties waiting. More of a stunt, I'd say, than proving any practical point about air travel."

Ben sat upright in his chair. "When the Wright brothers were flying down at Kitty Hawk twenty years ago, people said that was a stunt, too. Someone has to start everything—even if it does look like a crazy trick."

Dick Wood looked at Ben critically. Then a slow grin spread over his face. "Don't you fellows get mad at me. If I weren't interested, I wouldn't be here. And since when has it become a crime for a man to argue in Alaska?" He dug into his pocket and pulled out a checkbook. "Let's get started. What's this contraption going to cost?"

Ben tried to stop the wild pounding of his heart. He licked his dry lips, stuttered, then tried again. "Right after the war, those Jennies were selling as war surplus for as a low as fifty dollars crated. Now they're lots higher, maybe six or seven hundred dollars. And freighting them up here would be high—maybe another seven hundred dollars."

"Don't we know it," Thompson snorted.

"And then we'd need a field and a hangar, also a mechanic—" He faltered when he saw Dick Wood hesitate. But his heart leaped up again when the pen touched the check and started moving.

"We'll start with a thousand dollars," Wood said as Ben finished. He cleared his throat. "Don't know if I'm starting on a new business venture or throwing money into the furnace. But it'll be interesting." He looked up sharply. "Anything wrong with you, Ben? You're not sick or anything, are you? You look white."

Ben nodded his head. "Sure, I'm sick. I'm so happy, I'm shaking. I wish I could feel this sick all the time!"

The winter dragged by slowly for Ben. He tried to keep himself occupied in preparing for his classes in English, science and for his duties as basketball coach. Usually he was quiet and reserved, but the forty-eight pupils of the red frame high school knew that just one question about aviation was enough to start the tall teacher talking volubly.

His mind was always on the letter that had gone south, requesting shipment of a Curtiss JN-4 airplane from a used-airplane salesman in Kansas. He called so many times on Dick Wood and Wrong

Font Thompson, asking if a reply had been received, that he became self-conscious and resolved not to bother the two men again.

Whenever possible, Ben dressed warmly and slipped out to explore the few roads radiating from the town, trying to absorb as much of the surrounding terrain as he possibly could.

He had to admit to misgivings. Fairbanks was surrounded by low hills. Leaden clouds were always prominent on the horizon. Small-boled birch trees —each one like a deadly arrow ready to pierce any plane seeking a landing—were thick on the land. Countless small lakes, covered with ice and looking like white scabs on the face of the browned tundra, were waiting to confuse any flier. The streams that existed in endless numbers, all deceptively frozen and looking alike, corkscrewed over the countryside, doubling back and forth in small loops until they nearly touched, then arcing away again.

Ben remembered the hardships of his early flying days when he had so much difficulty with his cross-country training flights in California.

"Maybe," he said to himself as he hiked along the frozen dirt road, "if Wood and Thompson knew how I nearly failed that cross-country checkout, they might not want to trust me with their airplane!"

Everything he saw about the city, he linked for

possible use with flying. One morning, as he walked to school across the iron bridge that spanned the frozen Chena Slough, he noticed a crowd gathered around one of the big girders. Shouldering his way through, he saw one of the grammar-school students crouched in an awkward position, his face pressed close to the girder.

"What's wrong?" Ben asked. "What happened?"

"Danged fool kid," a bystander told him, "stuck his wet tongue against the iron, and now he's froze fast. They'll fix him up in a hurry, though."

From one of the stores, a merchant ran out carrying a small tumbler of warm water. He leaned over the boy and poured the water over his tongue. The little fellow pulled his head back cautiously. Suddenly he was free. Sobbing, he leaped to his feet and ran down the street.

"Ain't the first time it's happened. Can't seem to get it into the heads of these kids their first winter up here—you just can't touch bare skin to metal in these cold spells. Danged thing freezes tight in a flash. Try to pull away, and it rips the skin right off. Frightful, that's what it is. Frightful."

All the way to the school Ben puzzled over the happening. Always his mind drifted back to flying. How could a mechanic service a plane in Alaska during the winter? How could he lift a wrench, without having the skin of his hand freeze to the metal? How could he repair an engine, twist a fuel line or change a wheel, without risking the loss of his fingers?

"Maybe it's impossible," Ben said to himself. "If we ever do get a plane up here, we'll be able to fly it only in the summer. We'll have to do like a lot of people here do with their automobiles—store 'em in garages for the winter, drain the oil, deflate the tires—and just forget they exist until the weather decides to act decent again."

Late in March an acknowledgment of the airplane order was received. There was a flurry of excitement around Fairbanks, then interest ebbed again. Ben became restless, nervous. He wrote long letters to his family in North Dakota, telling of his hopes and discouragements.

Ben found it impossible to sleep soundly. With the weather moderating, he slipped from his room in the Alaska Hotel late at night and paced restlessly on the roads leading from Fairbanks. Time and time again he walked down to the little railroad station, waiting for the occasional freight trains that hooted mournfully to rest after the long haul up from Seward and Anchorage. He scanned the lines of cars, trying to find one that would be loaded with oblong crates.

But no airplane arrived and the months crept past.

In April the terrible cold loosened its grip on Fairbanks, although each night the temperature sagged well below the freezing point. The rumble of mining activity began to be heard as the prospectors prepared to go out to the gold creeks ringing the town. The harsh spring thaws buckled the roads, broke pipes and twisted the lines of the Alaska Railroad in long, weirdly waving patterns.

Ben waited with growing despair through the month of May. School was rushing to a close, and still the plane had not come. Worse, in the great surge of mining activity that came with each spring, the town had seemingly forgotten the lonely young schoolteacher who waited for a plane to take him into the air. People no longer stopped him on the street to ask for news. Even the schoolchildren, looking forward anxiously to their vacation, had tired of asking questions about aviation.

Ben had never felt so lonely. By this time he was convinced that the plane had been lost in transit yet he was too proud to ask Dick Wood to write again asking that the shipment be traced.

In June of 1923, when the sun was strong on the newly reborn town of Fairbanks, he stood in his classroom and watched the students stream off for the summer holidays. He said good-by to Mr. Keller and to Esther Smith and Hannah Sponheim, the other staff teachers.

"What are your plans, Ben?" Already they had forgotten the promised airplane. Or, charitably, they looked upon it as one of the many wild schemes devised during the biting cold of a winter's night.

"Haven't decided yet," he answered truthfully.

He walked to the narrow bridge spanning the swift-flowing Chena Slough. Behind him heavy trucks rumbled back and forth in a ceaseless round of activity. He heard the whistle of an inbound train and stared disconsolately at the cars easing into the station.

A truck screeched to a halt on the narrow bridge and the driver leaned over to yell, "Hey, Ben, there's a telegram waiting for you at the Signal Corps office!"

He ran the short distance, burst into the office, claimed the telegram and read it while his hands trembled.

AIRPLANE SHIPMENT LEFT SEATTLE TO-DAY STEAMER NORTHWESTERN. WILL ARRIVE SEWARD TWENTY TWO JUNE. PLEASE MAKE NECESSARY ARRANGEMENTS RAILROAD SHIPMENT SEWARD TO FAIRBANKS.

Ben walked slowly from the little office out into the open air. He tried to appear unconcerned, but when he was sure no one was watching, he looked up at the sky, a slow smile spreading across his face.

"She's on her way," he whispered. "I'm going to fly."

CHAPTER 7

"Easy, now. Easy. Don't drop 'em."

The crates had completed the bumpy journey from the depot, over the bridge and along the dirt street paralleling the slough. Ben watched while they were eased to the ground in the ball park. Grouped around him were Ira Farnsworth, the mechanic from the town garage, Dick Wood, Wrong Font Thompson and an assortment of curious schoolchildren.

"What's the first thing you do when you try to put an airplane together, Ben?"

Ben grinned slowly and ran a hand through his tousled blond hair. "Best thing is to pull these crates apart and see what's inside."

Half a dozen men leaped on the crates, yanking at nails, cutting wire straps, pulling boards backward with a tremendous screech. The motor was uncovered, the fuselage and the wings. Soon the infield was littered with an array of parts that were spread around like remnants of an explosion.

Dick Wood looked at the pieces dubiously. "It's

going to be harder to put all these things together than it will be to fly the airplane!"

"Here's a wheel," Thompson called from the first-base line. "Shall we start from the wheels up, or build back from the tail?"

Ben shook his head. "Here's a time when a pilot wishes he were a mechanic." He thought momentarily of Hank Robinson and his eyes clouded. "Ira," he said, "we'll have to let you call it. Even if you've never seen an airplane before—you'll have to put this one together."

All of Saturday and Sunday the group toiled over the assembly. Thompson approached Ben and spoke diffidently. "Didn't tell you this before, Ben. Folks down at Nenana, they're having a big celebration on the Fourth of July, Wednesday—well," he concluded sheepishly, "I kind of told them you'd fly down and do a few tricks. They've sold tickets and things like that."

Ben juggled the engine piston in his hand. "Short notice. But we'll try."

The plane grew like a child's toy taking shape. The undercarriage and wheels were affixed to the fuselage. The wings were mated to the body and the strong guy wires laced between. The heavy motor was lifted into the nose of the ship and bolted into position. The connections were made to the fuel lines. Cables led from the stick out to the ailerons and back to the rudder.

Sunday night Ben was unable to sleep. For a while he paced about his room in the Alaska Hotel, then quietly slipped outside and walked down to the ball field. Approaching the nearly completed plane, he remembered his primary training days back at Mather Field in California. Six years had passed, yet he was able to recall the ten hours of dual instruction he had received, the twenty-four hours of solo flying and the sixteen hours of cross-country flying he had completed. He remembered the names of his instructors and the names of the students who had crashed and been killed. Most of all he remembered Hank Robinson.

There was a shaded spot behind home plate, and he went over and stretched out on the grass and fell asleep.

"Hey, you, Ben! Wake up. We've got work to do!"

It was Ira Farnsworth who shook him awake.

"You run up to the café and get a bit of breakfast, Ben. I'll get started. Stop by the garage and bring my set of socket wrenches, will you?"

But Ben was too excited to eat. He brought back the wrenches and with Ira and others helping, he wrestled the bulky gas tanks into position to the rear of the pilot's cockpit.

"Get this loaded with gas," Ira grunted, "and you'll be lucky if she lifts you, Ben, let alone any passengers."

Ben wiped the perspiration from his forehead. "Not as bad as you make out, Ira. She'll lift four hundred pounds besides me."

"Ain't room for but one passenger," Ira repeated stubbornly.

"True—but after we get in business, we're going to move this gas tank up above the top wing. That'll let us carry four passengers—if we can find them!"

There were still a hundred details to be taken care of before the plane could be airborne. The hours slipped by, the sun high and hot in the sky, and still the ship was not ready. Wrong Font Thompson appeared on the field looking doleful, the afternoon edition of the paper clutched in his hand. "Yesterday, I told 'em in my column that you'd surely fly today, Ben. 'Tomorrow, sometime,' I said, 'the flier intends to fly over our town. He is having his troubles getting ready on time.'" He looked sideways at Ben. "But not real trouble, eh, Ben? You'll surely get her up today?"

"Sure."

But six o'clock came and the ship was still not ready to fly. Two baseball teams, the Has-beens and the Comers, moved onto the field to start a game, and the airplane was shoved ignominiously into the outfield.

By eight o'clock the game had ended and a few curious spectators wandered down to the little group about the airplane, then wandered off again. Far away the yelping of the tied sled dogs could be heard in the strange sun-filled stillness of Fairbanks on a calm July night, for this was the period of almost complete daylight in the Far North.

Suddenly Ben straightened. He looked the plane over carefully, standing back and tilting his head.

"All right," he said quietly, "she's ready. We'll push her up to home plate and I'll take off down toward left field. That'll take me over the slough in a hurry just in case."

"Ben," Wrong Font Thompson asked, "you're going to warm up the motor first, aren't you? All the pictures I see . . ."

Ben nodded his head. "She'll either go—or she won't. There's nothing halfway with these motors."

The men strained at the wings, rolling the light ship over the hummocks that crowded the outer fringes of the ball park. They stood in silence while Ben climbed into the cockpit. He waited a moment, testing the rudder and the stick, looking back over his shoulder to watch the ailerons flipping in response to his movements. Then he nodded to Ira Farnsworth standing by the propeller. The mechanic pulled and grunted and the propeller came over, the motor chugging and dying. Ben nodded again. Once more Ira spun the prop, and once more the motor chugged and failed.

But on the third try it came to life with a sputtering roar.

Ben held the throttle, his head cocked forward, listening. As he pulled the throttle outward, the motor leaped as though it had been jabbed with a pin. The entire fuselage trembled; the upper and lower wings fluttered and the entire ship lunged forward, straining against the protective grasp of the men who leaned their weight against it.

He made a last check on the controls. Then he held his hand aloft and nodded to Ira Farnsworth.

"Let's go!" Ira yelled.

While everyone pushed, Ben gunned the motor. The Jenny started to roll, the men at the wings running awkwardly behind, still pushing, yelling encouragement. Out past the pitcher's mound the Jenny lurched its way, picking up speed, ramming forward toward second base.

Ben took his time. He was more concerned with the safety of the men running along with the plane than he was for his take-off. He never for a moment doubted the response of the trembling ship when he was ready to give it the last command to leap into the air. The hummocks on the outfield were an obstacle, but he kept glancing from side to side, waiting until the breathless pushers had stumbled safely away from the sharp-edged tail surfaces.

As Ben saw the last helper fall away, he fed full

power to the roaring motor. The ship leaped into the outfield, bounced, skidded and lifted. He kept the nose down, down, down, resisting the upward pull, skimming over the fence, lifting slightly over the fast-running waters of the Chena Slough, brushing over the line of alders on the far bank. He turned slightly to avoid the hospital, keeping the ship in its gradual climb over the flatland on the far side of the slough. His hand was firm on the stick, as though he were restraining an excited thoroughbred horse. Clear of any obstacles, he listened intently to the even throb of the motor. He touched the rudder bar slightly, sensing the ready response of the ship, then countered with an alternate move.

When he had gained sufficient altitude, he shoved the nose down, and the wind whipped through the open cockpit as the frail ship picked up speed. He waited, full of confidence, as the ground raced upward to meet him, the brown of the tundra and the pale green of the countless water pockets growing larger and larger. At the last moment he pulled at the stick and almost bodily lifted the Jenny in a sharp climb, thrusting the nose straight at the blue sky and reaching for the heavens. At the peak of the climb, satisfied that this plane was equal to any of those he had handled in his training and barnstorming days, he circled lazily over the town, looking down at the little figures who were scurrying from the stores on Front Street and the log homes scattered about, all of them gesticulating, pointing toward the plane.

At nine o'clock in the evening, the sun was still high on the horizon. In its journey about the sun, the earth was tilting to the glowing ball of fire and all the northern latitudes were bathed in the direct scorching rays. A slight dusk would come shortly after midnight, then, less than an hour later, the sun would edge over the eastern horizon ready for the start of a new, hot summer day.

He could see the red school building plainly, then the ball field came in view, with the tight knot of men standing, white-faced, looking up at his plane. Impulsively Ben kicked the rudder and the ship went into a sharp turn. He hit the stick and the nose dived downward. He felt like shouting in exultation.

He took for his target the iron bridge spanning the Chena Slough, and dove at it as though he intended to destroy the plane and himself against the tangle of steel girders. Down, down the plane screamed, Ben yelling encouragement. At the last moment he pulled out of his dive, roared over the span and then sent the Jenny upward in a wide, sweeping arc. Not satisfied, he came back to his target again, but made his dive steeper this time, pulling out within a few scant feet of the flat surface of the slough, holding the ship steady and roaring forward under the low steel bed of the bridge.

The buildings on the south side of the bank went by in a brown daub of color; the boats tied to either side of the slough flashed behind in a white and green streak. He yanked on the stick, pulled tight around the twin smokestacks of the Northern Commercial Company steam plant, and flipped the plane over on its back.

For twenty minutes Ben subjected the willing Jenny to every maneuver he had ever learned, even putting in a few additions that he invented on the spur of the moment. Never once did the ship falter. He was in complete control of the little cloth-covered plane.

Finally Ben quieted himself. He felt almost guilty at the display he had put on, but he told himself that he was only trying to discover bugs in the plane. He held his altitude at three thousand feet, turning in slow circles above the town, listening to the steady drone of the motor, the even feel of the ship as it responded to slight pressures on the controls. He wanted to look around at the surrounding countryside. Soon, he knew, his life might depend on knowledge he would acquire of the scant landmarks in the baffling monotony of the tundra below him. He started to trace the winding course of the Chena down to its meeting with the Tanana River, miles beyond Fairbanks.

He tried to memorize the thousand-odd pockmarks of water that dotted the uneven surface of the tundra, and he looked more intently at the long, low range of hills far to the north of the town.

Then he remembered the group waiting impatiently at the ball field. He put the ship into a turn, a slow glide, then let it fall as gently as a guided feather down to the rutted grass of the field. The rubber tires touched, bounced slightly, touched again and rolled unevenly over the humps to the dusty yellow of the diamond.

The men came running and Ben cut the motor quickly. He had witnessed gruesome accidents with whirling propellers at the training fields.

"Ben, it was terrific." Dick Wood stretched his hand up and tried to pull himself level with the cowling. "If I hadn't seen it with my own eyes, I wouldn't have believed it. Although," he continued, as he reached out to Ben as the latter climbed down from the plane, "there were a couple of times when I thought the Farthest North Airplane Company was going out of business in a hurry. How do these ships stay in one piece when you throw them around like you did?"

"They'll take that and more," Ben reassured him. "I'm not afraid of what happens up in the air. It's this field I'm worried about." He walked away from the plane and stared thoughtfully at the little ridges that crisscrossed the outfield. "We'll have to beef up the wheel struts. Might be better if we did a little pick-and-shovel work out here in trying to fashion some kind of runway." He turned anxiously to Dick Wood. "You think the ball team would mind if we—"

"Mind? We might be saving some left fielder a broken leg if we did just that, Ben. They won't mind. In fact," he said confidentially, "we might even get these fellows down to help. What else, Ben? Anything about the plane, the motor, you want fixed before we start hanging up signs telling folks we're in business?"

"Yes, Dick. She's left-wing heavy. Take up a couple of turns on that left turnbuckle."

"Wait a minute, Dick," Wrong Font Thompson interrupted, waving a sheet of paper in his hand. "Let me at that young fellow first. You realize," he boomed to all assembled about, "this is only the third time we've had an airplane flying over Fairbanks? You folks realize you've just witnessed history? Maybe the first time an airplane's ever been assembled and flown out of a field in Alaska? Why, believe me . . ." He stopped hastily. "Excuse me, Ben, this was to be an interview, not a speech. Listen here, listen to what I've written . . ."

At nine o'clock in the evening, on the 3rd day of July, 1923, Professor B. C. Eielson went aloft in his airplane. His machine had never been flown; the engine had never been turned over; the wires and wings never tested off the ground. He tied the parts together, gave the propeller a whirl and went up.

Ben grinned. "If people are going to remember, maybe you ought to get the initial right—it's C.B., not B.C."

Thompson shook his head dolefully. "Just like a cub reporter—I'm so excited. Did I spell the last name wrong, too?"

"Wouldn't be the first time." Ben looked around impatiently. "Let's get some shovels and . . ."

"Let's get some sleep," Ira Farnsworth objected. "We've been working since last Friday. If I don't get home soon, my family'll think I took off for Siberia in this here airplane."

The plane was pushed to a far side of the field, and when one of the group volunteered to act as guard, Ben walked uptown with his friends. Only when he sat on the stool in the Model Café did he realize how tired he was. He ate hastily, excused himself and went back to his hotel room. Pulling down the blinds to shut out the light, he kicked off his boots and fell across the bed. Within seconds he was fast asleep.

Early the next morning he was awake and down at the field. He was relieved to see the plane intact. For some reason he could not get rid of the feeling that the airplane, sitting so quietly with its stilled motor, was unreal, that it would be gone in a few hours, a few days.

He was tempted to overcome that feeling of impending loss by taking the ship up again, stunting wildly over the town to show that the plane was real, that he was unafraid. It had been a classic antidote during his training days. But the sight of the bumpy, uneven baseball field that had been selected as a site for the operations of the Farthest North Airplane Company chased all other thoughts away. He hunted a shovel and began to scrape at the treacherous hummocks.

One after another the little band of stockholders appeared at the field carrying garden tools. Groups of young men and boys showed up and were enticed into the uninviting work with vague hints of possible rides.

After lunch Dick Wood looked impatiently at his watch. "Those people at Nenana are waiting for us, Ben. They've sold a lot of tickets at one dollar a head to people wanting to watch you do your tricks with the airplane. Hate to disappoint them. Bad publicity for the company."

Ben swung harder on his shovel. "Another hour, Dick, and we'll be ready."

At four o'clock in the afternoon the Jenny was poised again for take-off. Ben was at the controls. Dick Wood, trying to conceal his excitement, climbed awkwardly into the rear seat, jamming his big frame into the tight opening. He leaned forward and spoke to Ben. "You promise now—you'll let me off first in Nenana before you try any shenanigans? I don't want my insides all scrambled up like an egg."

"I promise. Hold on, now. Here we go!"

Ben gave the signal to the man at the propeller, and once more the Jenny roared with life. He waited a few minutes for the motor to run through a crescendo of sound, then nodded to those grouped about the plane. Almost at once it began to leap forward. The wheels rolled on the new runway, and though there were still many rough spots and the menacing woodpiles on either side, the little ship leaped into the air and sped over the slough.

Dick Wood waited until the group dropped away. Then, with one hand clapped over his hat and the other clutching his light coat tightly about his neck, he cupped his hands and yelled, "By golly, she's a wonder! She's a three-day jumping wonder!"

Ben nodded, grinning. He looked over the side of the plane, picking out the winding run of the Chena Slough immediately below, and in a much straighter line, the steel track of the Alaska Railroad. He shouted and motioned downward, tilting the plane slightly so that Dick Wood could see far below. A train moved slowly on the track, black smoke belching from the locomotive that pulled a string of passenger cars.

"Excursion train going down to Nenana!" Ben yelled to Wood.

The older man nodded. He called to Ben, "Man, wouldn't I—"

The words were cut off as the nose of the ship dropped and the plane began to hurtle down straight toward the train. Dick Wood grabbed his hat and slid down out of sight.

Down, down the airplane sped until it was almost level with the tracks. Then Ben gave a quick flip to the stick and lifted the ship until it was only a few feet above the speeding train. He flew the length of it, banked and turned, and came back, window-high, along the train. He repeated this twice, lifting his hand in greeting to the scores of faces jammed against the windows, then kicked the ship upstairs. "Dick!" he yelled. "Dick—"

But all he could see in the rear cockpit was a wisp of hair standing straight in the slip stream. Dick Wood had lost his hat and was crouched in the bottom of the cockpit, determined that nothing else would go over the side.

Ben kept looking ahead. The railroad bent slightly north, seeking the protective gully of Goldstream Creek as it slipped between the low hills just beyond the Tanana River. He told himself he would waste precious gasoline if he followed the wandering course of the river rather than streaking in a beeline for Nenana only forty air miles away. He wished he had studied the available maps just a bit more closely before taking off. But, he reasoned, Nenana was at the foot of the bluff at a point where the big Tanana River made an abrupt right-angle turn. He couldn't possibly miss it.

In the still evening air he should be able to pick up smoke columns rising from the cooking fires of the little village. And there, far to the left, were the thin signals he was looking for. He eased the plane about, leaning to the headwinds that were beginning to buffet the plane. Mentally he was already planning his landing, reassuring himself that the ball park at Nenana would be no worse than that at Fairbanks.

The plane bored on ahead. Ben looked over the side, for he was almost above the smoke columns. Surely, he thought, the town should soon be in sight, the sharp drop of the bluff would be evident. But nearly an hour had passed since the take-off from Fairbanks, far more time than he should have consumed on the short flight. He began to feel uneasy, nosing the plane over and going down in a steep glide to check the smoke columns that had signaled him to this spot.

As the ground swelled into larger proportions, he was able to get a clear view of the smoke columns. His heart sank. The smoke rose from the chimney of an isolated Indian cabin. A river was below, but the bluff that would identify Nenana, the unmistakable view of the railroad bridge spanning the river, was nowhere in sight.

"I've done it again," Ben whispered to himself. "I'm lost. My first trip out—and I'm lost!"

CHAPTER 8

Ben looked sharply around to see if Dick Wood had discovered their predicament. But the banker gave no sign of concern. He was still hunched far down in his seat, the white of his knuckles visible on the cockpit cowling.

Too late Ben realized the inexcusable error he had committed on his first cross-country attempt in Alaskan flying. Flying low, he discovered not one river, but two; and even as he watched, still a third came into view. And the land was flat as a pancake, marshy, dotted with literally thousands of bodies of water, most of them scarcely larger than the plane which flew over them.

Suddenly he saw the gleaming rails of the Alaska Railroad beneath him. If he guessed wrong as to the direction he should take now, he said to himself grimly, he'd be heading down to Anchorage and an inevitable crash landing in the northern foothills of the Alaska Range. But with the sun in the western skies to guide him, he wheeled the ship about, held within three hundred feet of the tracks and bored northward. He kept raising his eyes, and his heart beat faster as he saw the outlines of hills. There was the corkscrewing Tanana River, bigger by far than any of these other misleading streams he had faltered over.

Then he saw the bluff, the bridge spanning the river and the tight cluster of brown buildings. He lowered the ship swiftly, noting the crowds that had gathered, and rolled to a stop.

Dick Wood emerged from his hiding place in the rear cockpit. He turned and offered his hand to Ben. "Thanks, thanks for the most thrilling experience of my life, Ben." He paused for a moment, looking down in great satisfaction at the firm ground on which the plane rested. "And thanks for that side trip down to the Teklanika and Nenana rivers. Didn't know you meant to detour so far south."

Ben pretended not to hear. "That must be the reception committee coming out, Dick. Let's find out about getting some gas in this ship so I can get on with the show."

Nenana had been an Indian village known only

106

to a handful of prospectors who had used the Tanana as a water highway through Alaska. Then the coming of the railroad had swelled the population until more than four hundred people were crowded along the banks of the swift water. Prominent among the strangers who walked the muddy streets of the village were the steelworkers engaged in erecting the long railroad span across the Tanana, the last link before the final completion of the Alaska Railroad running from Seward four hundred and seventy miles into Fairbanks.

"And, Professor," the head of the reception committee said to Ben as he lugged five-gallon cans of gasoline over to the airship, "two, three weeks from today we're going to have the President of the United States himself here to drive in the golden spike and finish off the railroad. Tell you what, Mr. Eielson, we'd like to have you come back that day and do a few dipsy doodles for President Harding."

Ben kept his eye on the gasoline as it gurgled into the plane's tank. "President Harding's coming up to Fairbanks, too, and I understand they've made arrangements for me to put on a show up there."

"Humph! That Fairbanks is getting too big for its britches. Think it was New York the way they carry on. Tell you what, mister, we've got the railroad, too, and we've got coal mines down at Healey, and the river steamer just started operating from Nenana down the Yukon to Holy Cross seven hundred miles . . . oh, excuse me." He took the empty gasoline can from Ben and stalked away for replacement.

As Ben watched him leave, he stroked his chin thoughtfully. The railroad would play its part in opening up the interior of Alaska. The scheduled steamer service down the Yukon during the summer months was another great forward step for Alaska. What part would the airplane play in this new lease on life that was being given to the northern territory? And what part would he himself play? He looked to the sun-filled night sky as though he were trying to peer into the future.

The Athletic Park was jammed with spectators, each one clutching a ticket showing he had paid the admission price of one dollar to watch the newcomer on the Alaskan scene.

"Run 'er around the ball park a few times," the committeeman requested Ben. "Lot of these folks never saw a plane before. Me," he continued, swelling a bit, "I was over in France. Now there was some *real* fliers." He cleared his throat hastily when he saw Ben's face redden. "We've paid the price we agreed on to Mr. Wood—just in case, you know."

Ben nodded briefly. Just in case he crashed and killed himself. Well, he said to himself as he gave the signal to spin the prop, if he had listened too closely to the small voices that always spoke to him while he was flying, he would have lost courage during his first flight. He started the plane rolling, whipping it about smartly so that a vast cloud of dust swirled down on the committeeman who had talked too much. Maybe he ate dirt over in France, too, the— Ben cut off his thoughts abruptly. Had to keep his mind on the job. He taxied slowly around the field, giving the spectators a close look at the ship.

In a surge of civic pride, Ira Farnsworth had taken a paint brush and daubed in huge white letters the word FAIRBANKS on either side of the dun-colored canvas covering the fuselage. Within a few feet of Ben's face where he sat in the forward cockpit, the exhaust pipes of the motor, the only visible part of the growling OX-5 power plant, were pulsing with jets of thin blue smoke. The chunky wings were spread stiffly outward, round skids beneath the lower wing protecting the downward-dipping canvas cloth from disastrous contact with the rough ground. The tail of the plane, separated from the ground only by a short stiff skid, rode up and down like a rowboat in rough waters.

Finally Ben lined up with the runway that had been prepared, fed power to the motor and roared into the air.

He whip-stalled, performed Immelmann turns,

tail spins, loops and power spirals in an hour-long show that had the spectators, white-faced below, gasping with excitement. Not that Ben could hear them—he was alone in the plane, almost detached from the entire world. His stunting was instinctive. His moves of hand to throttle and stick, the movement of his feet on the rudder bar, were smooth and instinctive. He made sure that he kept the plane within full sight of the sea of faces upturned to him. He was complete master of the plane, yet one with it. When it dove, he felt as though he had plunged himself headlong from the heights of a mountain, possessor of some secret ability denied most other men.

When the plane climbed, with its propeller pointed almost straight up, Ben could feel the motion, partake of the straining, going through almost a physical effort in the reach for the sky. Everything faded in the rush of the wind and the scream of the motor.

He knew then that he would never again go back to schoolteaching, that he would fly until the day he died.

He shook his head, clearing his mind of the dream clouds that had been filling it. He saw that his gas tank was getting low. Time only for a few more thrills, and then he would be forced to land. He headed out to the Tanana River, still within sight of the spectators at the Athletic Park, flipped over on his back, flipped again, and roared across the ball field, outthrust wheels of the undercarriage almost touching the ground in a stunt known as "grass cutting." Then he took the ship up and up and up, nosed over and came in for the climax, a full-powered dive at a small house nestled at the end of the field. He cleared the low roof with inches to spare, shot upward, rolled over lazily and came in, fishtailing, settling to a gentle landing.

A roar of welcome went up from the spectators. But Ben did not hear it. He remained seated in the plane, behind the stilled motor, looking up to the sky.

The next afternoon he flew back to Fairbanks with Dick Wood, grimly holding to the long, but safe, route traced by the tracks of the Alaska Railroad. "If I have to learn my lessons like a homing pigeon," Ben said to himself, "I'm not going to get lost again—ever."

He had ample opportunities for going aloft. Big advertisements had been inserted in the *News-Miner*.

STARTING TODAY
TO TAKE PASSENGERS UP
$15.00
FIRST COME, FIRST SERVED
FARTHEST NORTH AIRPLANE COMPANY
C. B. EIELSON, AVIATOR

In another section of the newspaper was the advertisement:

TIME FLIES, WHEN WILL YOU?
FLYING LESSONS FROM THE
FARTHEST NORTH AIRPLANE COMPANY
YOUR CHOICE OF THE LONG COURSE
OR
THE SHORT COURSE

The customers for the fifteen-dollar flights were lined up at first base, the money fluttering in their hands. One after the other they climbed into the rear cockpit, and time and again Ben whipped the plane down the ball field, lifted into the air and circled over the town of Fairbanks. Those who waited longest were most rewarded, for Ben was utilizing every hop to become more and more familiar with the terrain in widening circles about the town.

He followed the erratic course of the Chena Slough as it twisted around the flatland surrounding Fairbanks. He tried to solve the jigsaw puzzle of the Tanana River, broken by hundreds of sand bars and islets as it slogged a path through the tundra country five miles south of the city. He logged in his memory the straight sweeps of the graveled Richardson Trail leading west and south from the town on the long run down to Valdez. He made a permanent marker of the twisting dirt trail that led north before splitting toward Livengood on the left and Circle on the right. He began to make a mental inventory of the scores of little creeks hidden in the gullies of the low hills north of Fairbanks—Steel Creek, Engineer Creek, Goldstream, Happy, St. Patrick and Moose. Then, on succeeding trips, he swept over the endless tundra south of the town, trying to make sense out of the bogs and sloughs and aimless creeks that comprised the flat, swampy wilderness of grasses and bushes.

Nothing in all his previous navigating experience had been so utterly confusing as the terrain upon which he now looked. The streams in particular, usually almost as reliable a guide for a pilot as a pair of railroad tracks, seemed to go out of their way to add to the confusion of the baffling Alaskan landscape. They seemed to take delight in corkscrewing, in doubling back in small loops until the loops nearly touched, then arcing away again.

Ben wondered, with dismay, what these same landmarks which he was trying so painfully to memorize would look like when the snows of winter had fallen and completely masked them.

Winter? He shook himself. This was July. Winter was at least three months away. Time for plenty of flying before those lakes below would be covered with ice. He leaned the plane far over on its side, grinning as the passenger behind let out a short yelp of fright, and went into a long glide to the field.

He was almost savage in his impatience with himself, in his fierce determination to learn the topography of the surrounding country so that he would be able to return to Fairbanks regardless of any tricks his compass might play on him. During the initial weeks in which the little plane was in the air over Fairbanks, the weather was almost perfect. The skies were clear, the sun almost a continual visitor, with only brief shades of dusk appearing between midnight and two in the morning, then slightly longer as the summer grew older.

And Ben was grateful for the clear skies. Though he admitted it to no one, he always feared a recurrence of his secret weakness, a tendency, a fatal tendency, to become too easily lost.

He drove himself like a schoolboy cramming for an important examination. With a few exceptions, he was the first man ever to look down on the weirdly different terrain of interior Alaska, and he was determined that he would burn into his mind every creek, every slough, every river, mountain and hill of the vast, forbidding land that slipped by under the wings of his trembling ship.

The sight-seeing hops about the city were tremendously lucrative, and the cost of the little ship was paid off in ten days. Then the lines of eager people who wanted to go aloft for short hops dwindled. Commercial ventures must be secured to keep the plane flying in the Alaskan skies.

On Sunday afternoon, the fifteenth of July, less than two weeks after Ben had lifted the plane into the air for the first time, President Harding and members of his cabinet arrived in Fairbanks for a whirlwind twenty-hour visit. The President had previously dedicated the railroad bridge down at Nenana, officially opening the long-awaited Alaska Railroad. During the President's stay, Ben took his ship up and did every stunt that he had ever performed. Late on Monday afternoon, in a convoy of automobiles, the presidential party left for the trip down the Richardson Trail to the seacoast and their waiting steamer. From the air Ben watched the dust of the caravan wending its way southward. He was vaguely disappointed, yet he could not exactly define his disappointment. He had wanted to meet the President; he had thought that Wrong Font Thompson's glowing descriptions of the prowess of "Our Ben" would have aroused the President's curiosity.

"Shucks," he whispered to himself, "what would you have done if he had asked you to come meet him? Shake his hand? Offer him a ride? Maybe you think he'd pin a medal on you. Huh!"

So he hid his hurt, laughing at his own foolishness, and brought the plane in for a landing. He felt like a boy who had done handsprings to attract attention and then slunk out of sight when no one noticed him.

But someone had. Dick Wood was waiting to introduce him to a portly stranger.

"We're in business, Ben," the banker said, "real business. This is Mr. Roth, attorney for the Stewart and Denby mines over on Stewart Creek. They've had a breakdown and every hour is costing them money. Roth wants you to fly over today with the machine parts and to pick up the mail that's been piling up there for the past month. Take six days to go in over the trail. Figure you could fly over in an hour."

Ben hesitated. "What about a landing field?"

"Fellows at the mine heard about you—they've already hacked out a good strip."

Ben nodded his head. "Let's go look at the map."

"You won't need a map, Professor Eielson—excuse me, Lieutenant. I'll be glad to lead you there."

Ben grinned slightly at the new title. Wrong Font had been busy telling his newspaper readers about Ben's background. Then Ben looked sharply at Lawyer Roth. "Are you making the trip with me?"

"Yes."

"How much do you weigh?"

"What?"

"How much do you weigh?"

116

"Two hundred. Two hundred and five pounds."

"If you and the machine parts don't gross over four hundred pounds, fine. If you do, something will have to be left behind. Figure it out. And we'll still need a map."

"Lieutenant," the lawyer protested, "I know this country like the back of my hand. I could guide you into Stewart Creek blindfolded."

"Ever seen it from the air?"

"Of course not."

"That's what I mean. Get the map."

He traced the route carefully. With no head winds, and the Jenny's motor turning over smoothly at eighty miles an hour, the flight to the mining claim on Stewart Creek should take less than eighty minutes. Ben shook his head. The margin of safety was too slim. He retraced his route on the map, showing a dog leg to Munson where an opportunity for emergency landing was waiting, also a supply of gasoline if that should be necessary. There might be head winds, he told himself, so there were more reasons why he could not take any unnecessary risks.

Roth looked over his shoulder and snorted. "Dangest way I ever saw to take an airplane someplace. Thought you fellows took off like the birds and flew straight lines!"

Ben forced a smile. "How many days did it

take you to get to Stewart Creek—going in over the trail?"

"Five, maybe six, depending on what we were packing in."

"Get aboard. I'll have you there in less than two hours."

The heavily laden ship took off sluggishly, barely clearing the row of birch trees down by the Chena Slough. Ben treated the Jenny gently, letting it climb gradually to altitude, feeding gas to the laboring motor in just the right quantities to get maximum performance with the least amount of gasoline used. He was extremely alert, checking each stream as it flowed past under the trembling wing of the plane. Twice he doubted himself and felt a cold sweat of apprehension. He was on the verge of turning around to shout at Roth and ask for help in identifying landmarks. But he held back, deliberately taking the plane in a wide circle to return to a known check point, then starting forward again on the sure process of identification.

"One thing," Ben promised himself softly, "I'm not getting lost. Not if it's the last flight I ever make."

He heard a wind-whipped cry from the rear cockpit and saw his passenger crouching, pointing down excitedly to the right.

Smoke curled from a cabin chimney. Raw earth was heaped in thick piles beside holes gaping in

118

the ground. A tram car was poised on a set of wooden rails. Stewart Creek.

Looking over the side, Ben could see tiny figures running to a clearing, waving hats and towels. He let the Jenny ease downward gently, coming in low to pass over the landing strip. His heart sank. He couldn't land.

The miners had tried eagerly to prepare the single strip for its first airplane landing, but squarely in the middle of the narrow clearing were three tree stumps sticking up like jagged teeth.

Ben gunned the Jenny, lifting it high over the surrounding trees, and started to circle. He could see the consternation on the faces of men below.

Ben studied the terrain. There was a small sand bar less than a quarter of a mile from the mining camp, smooth and unperturbed in the swift running waters of Stewart Creek. Ben went down low, looking the sand bar over carefully. He circled again, wanting to be positive of his landing. Yet in the back of his mind he knew he had to land. There wasn't enough gas to allow him to retrace his course.

He made his decision and the plane responded instantly. The nose went down slightly, the wings outstretched, the roaring motor stilled. The plane seemed to reach out almost physically for the tiny strip of sand that was rushing up to meet it. The wheels touched at forty-five miles an hour, bounced, and the plane rolled to a safe landing. Less than three feet of water separated it from the shore. Already several of the miners were running through the underbrush, shouting greetings.

Lawyer Roth held out his hand. "Fine landing, Lieutenant. Fine landing. And," he continued, "it's only an hour since we left Fairbanks."

But he was pale and shaking as he clambered awkwardly to the ground.

CHAPTER 9

After the cargo and the mail were unloaded, Ben shouldered his way through the underbrush to the landing strip that had been prepared. "If you'll put a stick of dynamite under this stump—and this one and this one," he said, kicking at the offending toothpicks, "I'll be able to land the next time." He looked doubtfully at the runway, curving like the letter S between the close-pressing timber. He shrugged his shoulders. "Yes, I'll be able to make it."

He wanted to explain patiently to the eager miners who clustered around him that, in all fairness

120

to the Jenny and the pilot who must risk his life
with each landing and take-off, a minimum of fifteen hundred feet of fairly level land was an absolute necessity for a landing strip. But he remembered the twelve hundred feet that was serving his
purpose back at the ball park in Fairbanks, and he
knew the intense labor that had gone into this sor-
ry-looking replica of an airstrip. In Alaska nothing
conformed to accepted standards. Perhaps even airplanes would have to be tailored to fit the needs
of the scores of small communities that would
be demanding air service. The concept of an airstrip fifteen hundred feet long would have to be
discarded. In time, he told himself grimly, he'd
consider himself lucky to have one thousand feet
available for take-off.

"You'll be flying in regularly, Lieutenant?" Mr.
Roth asked anxiously. "Before we took off I dis-
cussed a contract with Mr. Wood about service
to the mine, delivering mail and supplies from
Fairbanks. You're quite sure the landing strip will
be satisfactory? That was the one condition Mr.
Wood insisted on."

Ben nodded. "Take those stumps out and it will
be. I'll check with Dick Wood when I get back.
We'll arrange a schedule."

With Roth again as his passenger, Ben flew back
to Fairbanks in seventy-five minutes. Head winds
buffeted the frail ship, and for the first time the

ninety-horsepower OX-5 motor seemed tiny and emitted a staccato cough as it fought the winds. Ben pulled the nose up and climbed to fifty-three hundred feet, steeling himself against the instinctive feeling of panic when he nosed upward through the clouds and lost sight of the ground. "I've got to learn," he said to himself. "I've got to start depending on this compass sometime. I can't always fly contact."

He held to his course, feeling the faint touch of perspiration under his helmet despite the cold blast of wind in the open cockpit. He watched his time and course carefully, sucked in his breath, then nosed over and slid down into the cloud bank. Down and down he dropped through the swirling, cottony mist, unable to see more than a few feet in front of the rattling motor. When he turned his head he could see his passenger squirm about and look anxiously toward him. Ben forced a smile, nodding his head cheerfully, and Roth turned away again.

"If he knew how scared I am," Ben said to himself, almost smiling, "he'd crawl forward and take over the controls."

But he held tight to his courage, his head cocked far to one side, straining to look through the white wisps of clouds. "A little more," he whispered, "a little more."

Suddenly the white of the clouds became gray, then the gray turned to brown, and there, twisting in a green ribbon against the tundra, was the Tanana River. Instinctively Ben gunned the motor almost as though he wanted to dive into the river, so great was his relief at having picked up a recognizable landmark. He flattened out, studied the twisting corkscrew intently and placed his position at the point where the Salchaket Slough poured into the Tanana River. His dogged persistence in memorizing every possible landmark in the Fairbanks area was paying off. He turned the small ship slightly to the left, sped low over the river to the Chena Slough, then fishtailed over the birches and rolled to a bumpy stop on the field.

The news of the first commercial airplane flight in Alaska went over the military telegraph wires stretched along the banks of the Yukon, leapfrogging to Unalakleet and St. Michael and Nome.

HISTORY WAS MADE TODAY IN ALASKA WITH THE FIRST COMMERCIAL PAYLOAD CARRIED ALOFT IN AN AIRPLANE. LT. BEN EIELSON PILOTED HIS PLANE FROM FAIRBANKS TO STEWART CREEK CARRYING PASSENGER, FREIGHT AND MAIL. MORE FLIGHTS ARE PLANNED IN THE NEAR FUTURE. AVERAGE SPEED ON JOURNEY MORE THAN A MILE A MINUTE.

The word went along the singing wires which sat on three-legged poles crossing the Wrangell

Mountains to Valdez, hurrying along the submarine cable to Sitka where the word was spread throughout all of southeastern Alaska.

CARL BEN EIELSON TODAY FLEW THE FIRST

MEN TOOK TO THE SKIES TODAY IN NORTHERN ALASKA FOR THE FIRST—

CARL EIELSON THE AVIATOR TODAY—

Carl Ben Eielson. Here was a strange name. But with each succcccding flight, each new thrill of expectation that swept over Alaska, the name lost its strangeness. Carl Ben Eielson, the flier. The words began to flow easily. People in Nome began to speak the name with a great deal of familiarity, and the citizens of Juneau spoke of Ben as though he were a speck in their own sky. "By golly, wonder could we get Ben Eielson to fly down here from Fairbanks? He's the man could do it, you know."

And they would walk to their wall maps and look knowingly at the vast expanse of mountain and tundra that marked the territory of Alaska.

Fairbanks to Juneau. Only six hundred miles by air. "That little plane of Eielson's could come down here in six hours," one of them confided to the

124

others. "What a difference in time that would make."

And they would look regretfully at the route Alaskans were forced to take between the two cities, going by boat across the wild, heaving waters of the Gulf of Alaska to Seward, taking the train up to Anchorage; resting a bit, then inching up to Curry, where the train made a night stop because the moose made it unsafe to travel in the darkness, and finally ending the long, weary journey at Fairbanks, nearly a full week away from Juneau.

None of this was lost on Ben. He was convinced that aviation would open up Alaska. "But one thing at a time," he cautioned Thompson, the newspaper editor. "We've got only one airplane, and our job now is to keep it in one piece. I'm having trouble ordering new spark plugs for the engine."

"Well, Ben, send a wire out to the States and order more! We got to keep you flying! There's towns and mining camps all over Alaska just begging you to come. People been moving more dirt building runways than any time since the big gold rush back in 1903."

Ben smiled, remembering the first attempt at runway building he had seen up at Stewart Creek. "I'll get off a wire for plugs and other parts," he agreed. "Manufacturers don't pay much attention. They all think we start hibernating up here after the Fourth of July."

An urgent message had come from Brooks, requesting that Ben fly there and land on the new airstrip without stumps that the miners had chopped out of the brush. He made the trip with mail and supplies despite a cold head wind from the north that tore at his exposed face. On the fast return trip, he brought back a sick miner who needed hospital care.

He continued his rigorous schooling, forcing himself to commit to memory every distinctive feature in the weird brown-and-green wilderness that flowed beneath the wings of the rattling plane. He suffered moments of uneasiness as he thought of the approaching winter when the snows would blanket the flatland and obliterate all the landmarks he had so painstakingly memorized. "Take care of that when it comes," he said to himself. "It'll be October —November—before there's any snow to worry about."

But he did worry. He worried constantly. The spare parts he had ordered did not arrive. He reminded himself glumly that it was only a very short time before the Jenny would be earthbound, unable to take to the skies because of some missing part.

The constant pounding on the rough fields where he landed had seriously weakened the landing struts. At each take-off and landing he braced himself, expecting the struts to collapse and the ship to flip over on its back.

But the Jenny, as though conscious of its new vital role in this transportation age of Alaska, kept roaring away, day after day through the warm summer season that yet remained.

As Ben gained more and more confidence, trusting the ship implicitly and himself with reservations, he began to grow impatient with the limited range of the small ship.

"Dick," he said earnestly to the banker in one of the rare moments when he allowed himself the luxury of voicing his innermost thoughts, "the ship and I are tied to a string that reaches out one hundred and fifty miles from Fairbanks—the amount of gas we can carry. If those folks out in the mining camps didn't have gasoline stocks, we couldn't even get out that far—seventy-five miles would be the limit—so we could have enough gas to fly back to Fairbanks. We need a bigger plane."

Wood nodded his head in sympathy. "One thing at a time, Ben. You're still a young man. We've been waiting a long while even for this little help you're giving us in getting around Alaska."

But Ben didn't hear. He kept staring off to the north, the dim unknown, the unexplored land far up to the Brooks Range, the bush country. Beyond was the Arctic Slope, and beyond that the ice field that led to the North Pole. Very dimly in his mind, he thought of Europe that was waiting on the other side of the Pole. This was the shortest way. North over the Pole to Europe. He shook himself awake.

"Maybe if we added extra gas tanks—" the banker said helpfully.

"That would cut down the pay load, Dick. No use flying in this country if we can't carry something to the people, or carry it out." Ben leaned against the plane, his head sunk forward on his chest, deep in thought. "I've seen scores of sand bars on the rivers where I could land, some of them three thousand feet long, twice the length we've got here."

Dick Wood nodded. "And all those mining camps are getting extra stocks of gasoline, Ben, hoping you'll be able to schedule flights in to them. That way you'll be able to spread out more from Fairbanks."

Ben didn't seem to hear. He dug his hands deep into his pockets, looking speculatively at the chunky OX-5 motor of the Jenny. "Read in the papers yesterday where Eddie Stinson flew the first non-stop flight between New York and Chicago. Eight and a half hours—with three passengers."

"That wasn't a Jenny he flew, was it, Ben?"

The flier shook his head shortly. "A Junkers. A big ship. Maybe . . ." He shook his head shortly.

"Maybe what?"

"Maybe we'll just have to get a bigger plane up here, Dick. Even the army De Havillands would be a big step forward."

Dick Wood cleared his throat. "I'm a businessman, Ben. I guess I'm a bit cautious. But we've got to take one step at a time. We've got an airplane. A good one. Let's show these Alaskans what it can do. Then maybe we'll talk about bigger airplanes." He turned and walked away.

That night in his hotel room, Ben wrote a letter to the Post Office Department in Washington, D.C. He had proven flying in Alaska was practical, but bigger planes were needed. "And," he continued, groping for just the right words, "it is the duty of the United States government to provide better mail service to Alaska, to provide the bigger planes that are needed." After he had walked downtown and mailed the letter, he had a momentary feeling of regret. For the first few weeks he had been flying in Alaska, he had sensed a calmness and a peace that had been denied him since the end of the war. He had the plane he had longed for. Why kick up a fuss?

But he wasn't satisfied with the Jenny and its short range of one hundred and fifty miles. He wanted to push out deeper into unknown territory. He was consumed with curiosity about the unknown and that was waiting to the north, beyond the Brooks Range, out in the bush country.

129

"Ben, wake up. Ben!"

He felt someone tugging at his shoulder, almost dragging him up bodily from the deep sleep that immersed him.

"What is it, Ira?"

"Emergency trip up to Circle City. Got to rush a pump up there before one of the mine shafts floods out entirely. Hurry up and get dressed. We'll be loading the pump into the cockpit—if it fits."

There was still a great deal of flying left in the little canvas-covered plane, Ben thought, as he climbed up to inspect the lashings on the pump, then settled into the forward cockpit. Almost daily he had been bouncing down the dirt path which was misnamed a runway in the ball park, flying off to some remote mining camp, the rear cockpit crowded with newspapers, mail, groceries, machine parts and occasional passengers. As the hours piled up on the laboring motor, he realized that any flight might prove to be his last, yet there was no thought of stopping while the weather remained clear and the motor kept churning.

Inevitably, the motor did quit, and it was on this flight to Circle City. He crabbed down to a landing on a sand spit in Birch Creek, pulled off the cover and stared morosely at the boiling radiator. Ben never pretended to know too much about the chunky piece of machinery that had been so dependable up until this moment. He knew it was wrong, for his life might depend on his ability to make simple repairs—yet he still studiously avoided becoming too well acquainted with the innards of the OX-5 motor.

He wished heartily that it was sacks of groceries he was transporting to Circle City, then he could measure his chances of survival against cans of beans and tomatoes and fruit. He could have fashioned a pack, taken some food and headed overland to Circle Hot Springs, less than twenty miles away. But when he looked at the unappetizing pump and then at the bewildering wilderness that waited on every side, he shook his head. A sudden vicious sting from a mosquito stabbed him. Ten, twenty, a hundred other mosquitoes rushed into the battle, each one seeking a choice spot and exacting a toll of blood.

"I'm getting out of here," Ben said to no one in particular. "I'm getting out—and I'm going to fly out!"

He swarmed over the motor of the Jenny, thrust his head under the cowling, running his hand speculatively over the maze of wiring. His hand touched the radiator and he jerked it back quickly, popping the burned skin to his lips to cool it. Cautiously he unscrewed the radiator cap and a vast cloud of steam squirted out.

He nodded wisely, as though he had discovered some great mechanical secret. He waited a few moments, fighting the waves of attacking mosquitoes, then dug out a new iron pot that Ira Farnsworth had made part of the equipment, and took trips down to the creek and back filling the parched radiator with cooling water. He leaned over into the cockpit, set the spark, then ran and chinned himself on the propeller. The motor roared into life. After one last whack at the swarming mosquitoes, Ben clambered back into the cockpit, gunned the plane into action and leaped for the sky.

Safely back in Fairbanks, he spent more and more time with Ira Farnsworth, the mechanic, learning the secrets of the impersonal chunk of metal that comprised the motor of the Jenny, the throbbing, rattling combination of pistons and belts and spark plugs and gears that enabled the collection of wood and canvas to lift into the air.

He was lucky, incredibly lucky. Alone in the skies, his ship responded to his every command, the motor kept turning over doggedly, though with more and more protest as the hours and the miles accumulated. All through August and September he continued his flights. He covered more than twelve thousand miles and was the object of admiration from the citizens of Fairbanks. "That Ben," one said, expressing a unanimous opinion, "he's the greatest flier in the world."

Not that Ben paid too much attention to the

praise. He knew his was the only plane flying in Alaska. Anything he did was news, a good topic of conversation. But he was aware of the flying that was going on in other parts of the world, of daring attempts at distance and altitude that were being made by other pilots in bigger and stronger ships.

And he wanted desperately to be one of them. He was ready to move forward in the world of aviation, and he wanted to move now.

Late in September, his moments of indecision were ended. When he walked out to the field he saw the small ice puddles that had formed during the night. He saw the workmen beginning to set up the protective wooden boxes around the exposed fire-plugs. The boxes would be filled with sawdust to keep the water from freezing during the bitter sub-zero weather that was fast moving in.

All about there were indications of coming winter. The waters of the Chena Slough flowed just as rapidly as ever, but with a frightened air, as though aware of the ice fringes that were forming each night along the banks of the stream. The grasses had browned and the birch trees were vivid with yellow leaves. When Ben took off on a flight he discovered that many of the dead pockets of water dotting the tundra country were covered with thin sheets of ice. The north side of the low hills beyond the town was lightly sprinkled with snow.

"Ben," Ira Farnsworth said to him glumly, "we got to call it quits. Any night now, the bottom is going to drop out of the thermometer. I've seen oil in this country, at fifty degrees below zero, get hard enough to kick. And you just got to keep oil running smooth if you want that there engine to keep turning over. And when the snows come—how you going to land with those thin bicycle wheels? Skis, that's what you need. I tell you, Ben, you got some serious problems if you think you're going to keep flying in this country during the winter."

Ben didn't reply. He kept looking up at the leaden sky, fingering the letter he had opened before leaving his room. It was from the Post Office Department in Washington, D.C., thanking Mr. Eielson for the letter he had written early in August. "No, the department could not consider furnishing an airplane for mail service in Alaska at this time. But, perhaps at a later date—"

"No, Ben," Ira continued, looking morosely at the little plane silhouetted against the gray background, "I'm afraid these here airplanes are going to be like everything else up in the interior—just bundle up at the first big freeze and go to sleep like a danged old bear. Maybe you'll get a few more flights, but that'll be it. We'll just have to shove this old plane into a hole until next April, May."

"No, Ira. You're wrong. We're going to fly in winter. Maybe not with this ship, but we're going to fly." He patted the Jenny affectionately. "When I get back from Stewart Creek this afternoon, we'll store the plane in the warehouse."

"That's not what I call flying—sitting in a warehouse."

Ben grinned in reply. "I'm leaving tomorrow on the train for Seward. I'm heading back to the States. When I come back, I won't be alone. I'll have with me the biggest and best airplane I can find in all the forty-eight states." He took a step away, then added, "I hope."

CHAPTER 10

To a man accustomed to flying, the train from Fairbanks back to the coast and the steamer down to Seattle were painfully slow. And to a man in a hurry, the trip seemed to stretch on forever.

Ben's journey across the northern tier of states was broken by his visit at Hatton, North Dakota, where he was welcomed by his father and his brothers and sisters. It was only after the initial excitement of greeting that Ben learned there was more to this meeting than a family reunion.

"Ben," his father said firmly, "we've been talking about this a lot while you were gone—and we want you to settle here in Hatton—maybe go in business with your brother Oliver."

"But Dad," Ben protested, "I've already got my business—the Farthest North Airplane—"

"That's just it," his father interrupted shortly, "we want you to get out of flying entirely. Go into farming or law—anything but those airplanes."

"But Dad, I can't give up flying. I like it. I'm going to spend the rest of my life flying."

Ole Eielson hesitated. "Well, son, if you must continue flying—why not here in the States?"

Ben studied his hands thoughtfully before replying. "Guess it's hard to say why a man likes one part of the country more than another. Like why our ancestors came here to Hatton rather than to Ohio or Kentucky. And those people up in Alaska —they're depending on me." He shook his head firmly. "I like Fairbanks. I want to return there, to fly there."

Finally, he said good-by to those who thronged about him, and stepped on the train that sped eastward to Chicago. He stayed for a few hours in the big city, walking restlessly from the railroad station through the Loop business district, then down to the waterfront of Lake Michigan. At

136

four in the afternoon he stepped aboard the Baltimore and Ohio train and tossed restlessly through the night as the wheels churned through Ohio and Pennsylvania. He was wide awake at midnight as the train slipped past the steel mills just beyond Pittsburgh. He could see the red glow of the furnaces and the cherry-colored ingots of steel that sent heat waves penetrating even into the train.

Long before dawn he was up prowling restlessly about the train. At Harpers Ferry he was the first one into the diner for an early breakfast. He had his bag packed and was waiting twenty minutes before the train pulled into the station at Washington.

Ben registered at a small hotel a few blocks from the station. Afterward he walked over to the Capitol Building where he had been a guard during his stay at Georgetown University. In the rotunda he met Dan Sutherland, starting his second term as Alaska's delegate to the United States Congress.

"Ben," the delegate said, greeting him warmly, "I might've known you'd be popping up here. Fact is, I should have sent you a wire. Might have saved you a trip."

"Why? Do you know what I—"

"Do I know what you want here in Washington? I sure do, young fellow. I've had people from the Post Office Department asking me all kinds of questions about you and your flying, what you know

137

about Alaska—you're becoming famous, Ben. That's the word. Famous."

"Did they say anything about the airmail contract?" Ben asked doggedly.

"What else do Post Office Department people talk about? Of course! They had some idea of letting out a short-term contract for a few flights between Nenana and McGrath—but I talked them out of that."

"You did?" Ben's face fell. "Don't you believe that airmail service is needed? Don't you think that we can fly in winter up in Alaska?"

"Ben, relax," the older man told him, putting his arm around Eielson's shoulder. "You're as tight as a drumstick. Sure I believe airmail service in Alaska is needed. What do you think was in the back of my mind when I urged you to go north a year ago? And who's been sticking pins in the Post Office Department ever since you got that plane of yours off the ground last July? Ben, believe me," he continued seriously, "you've been fighting hard to get the Government interested in flying the mail up in the territory—but don't forget there are a lot of Alaskans fighting with you."

"I'm sorry, Mr. Sutherland. I know what you say is true."

The delegate looked at Ben critically. "Tell you what. We'll set up an appointment with the Post Office people and iron out the details—then you take a holiday. You look worn out to me. Too much flying."

"But you said you talked them out of the Ne-nana-McGrath flights," Ben protested.

"That's right. Told them we wouldn't settle for anything less than the Fairbanks-to-Nenana flight. And that's what we got. A contract for ten round-trip flights, twice each month starting in January."

"What about the plane? What are we going to use?"

"De Havilland, with a four-hundred-horsepower Liberty motor. Couldn't ask much more, could we?"

"How soon will they send the plane? We've got a lot of work to do to get ready."

"Plane will be up there in plenty of time. These people aren't slow—just cautious. And, Ben—"

"Yes, sir?"

"About the money part of it. The department only wants to pay you two dollars a mile—that's less than half what the contractor's getting for taking the mail down by dog sled."

Ben shrugged. "If the Post Office Department only knew it, they missed a bargain."

"What do you mean?"

"I'd have flown that mail for nothing. Just give me the ship—and the chance to fly!"

Ben was back in Fairbanks long before the arrival of the plane the Government was providing.

He pored over maps of the three-hundred-mile

139

route between Fairbanks and Nenana, and talked with the dog-sled driver who made the mail run. He was worried, not about the plane or his safety, but about his penchant for getting lost. Winter had come quietly to Fairbanks. Light snow covered the ground. Each night the temperature plummeted far below zero.

When the plane finally arrived on the Alaska Railroad freight car, it was hauled on a sled to the Fairbanks ball field. The powerful Liberty motor, which would pull the De Havilland through the air at one hundred and fifteen miles an hour, was assembled after a great deal of debate on the positioning of the various valves and pistons.

"We'll have to pull those wheels and make some sort of skis," Ben said. He was excited, but he tried to conceal it. He asked Charlie Schiek, the local carpenter, to fashion skis. He watched as Charlie stood solemnly by the plane, intently studying the chunky wheels of the De Havilland and making tentative sketches on a piece of two by four. "I'll try, Ben," said the carpenter. "Haven't had much experience in this. Skis for an airplane? Who'd ever thought—"

A big white canvas curtain hung before the open front of the shed that housed the airplane. Ben walked away from the cluttered excitement, out to the still, silent cold that embraced the town. He walked down to the frozen Chena Slough, listening to the crunch of his shoes on the brick-hard ground.

It seemed so simple, the task that was before him. The De Havilland was a good plane, the mainstay of the United States Army since the close of World War I. And the Liberty motor was the finest, with more than four times the horsepower of the puttering collection of metal in the Jenny's OX-5 engine. The speed was increased nearly half again and the huge gas tanks placed forward of the pilot more than doubled the Jenny's puny range of one hundred and fifty miles.

The De Havilland was still boxy, but the first vestiges of streamlining were appearing on the ship. The forest of bracing wires between the two wings that featured the Jenny had disappeared, and the rear fuselage had begun to taper in more graceful lines.

This was the ship and this was the motor that would go a long way toward conquering the intolerable distances in Alaska. Yet inwardly Ben was uneasy.

He knew that when the time came to take off for McGrath, he would be flying close to death. He would get a telegraphed weather report from Mc-Grath before flight time, but it could easily change by the time he spanned the three hundred miles to the little town on the Kuskokwim River. There were less than a hundred human beings scattered over the distance between the two towns. If the weather remained good he might be able to follow the dog trail as a guide; otherwise, he would be forced to rely solely on his compass and good flying judgment in order to reach his destination. A forced landing, even if the plane remained intact, could mean certain death. For he was to take an airplane, the first ever flown in an Alaskan winter, over a region that was wild, lonely and menacing, perhaps the worst spot in the world.

Yet he never hesitated. If death had been a certainty, he would still have made the attempt, convinced that somehow he and his plane would outwit the certainty.

On the morning of February 21, 1924, with the temperature at a mild five degrees above zero, the ship was pushed out of the warm haven of the shed hangar. It stood awkwardly on its ponderous skis, almost as though self-conscious at the crowd that had gathered. Ben waited impatiently while a dog team was driven alongside the plane. There were speeches about the new era for Alaska, about the blazing of new sky trails, about the heroism of the intrepid pilot. But Ben never heard a word. He was so busy seeing to the stowing of the five hundred pounds of mail destined for McGrath that he was startled when a deep silence settled over the crowd and a voice sounded oddly, "Good-by, Ben."

There was a touch of sadness, almost as though he were going to his death.

But Ben was too busy to be concerned. He warmed the motor, racing it to full power, then throttling back. When he gave the signal and poured gas to the motor, he was dismayed when the ship, quivering violently, refused to budge. The skis had frozen fast to the thin snow. But a dozen helpers rushed to the wings, pushing in concert, and the two-winged plane lumbered down the runway, squirting snow from the awkward skis. The ship trembled violently. Ben rammed the throttle to full power, and finally the De Havilland, with a convulsive twist, rose into the chill air.

It was eight-forty in the morning.

The first leg of the journey, over to Nenana, passed without incident. He had made the trip along the Tanana River so many times that even now, with the landmarks hidden under a white blanket, he was still confident, sure of himself. Over the town, he banked to the left, setting his course southwest across the white wasteland. The Liberty motor roared smoothly. The stinging cold air flowed past the open cockpit. Over his left shoulder Ben could see the massive bulk of Mount McKinley more than a hundred miles away, calm, impassive. A loose tie rope from one of the mail sacks lashed about wildly in the slip stream. Under the sacks were stored emergency food supplies, snowshoes, a

143

gun and an ax. "Just in case," one of the onlookers had said at the take-off, "just in case that fellow smashes up the plane and has to find out what it means to walk for a change."

Perhaps the time would come when he would be vitally concerned with survival on the ground, but for the moment Ben's thoughts were only of the steady roar of the motor, the smooth handling of the ship as it raced across the Alaskan landscape at one hundred and fifteen miles an hour.

Ben dropped low over the scrub pine surrounding Lake Minchumina, the halfway point of the trip. He saw tiny black specks on the dog trail below, and pin-pointing on them, he roared over the astonished dog team and its driver who looked upward, startled, at this new apparition in the sky. Three hours and nine minutes away from Fairbanks, he wheeled over the town of McGrath and settled the ship on the frozen surface of the Takotna River. The entire population was on hand to scream a hoarse greeting as the De Havilland lurched to a stop.

Airmail service had come to Alaska. Twenty days by dog sled had been reduced to three hours and nine minutes by airplane.

And yet for Ben there was no sharing in the wild jubilation of those who thronged about him. There was always the next flight, the next turn of the propeller, the next take-off and the next landing.

He grinned shyly at those who pushed about him, thumping him on the back, crawling over the plane, but his eyes were lifted to the sky. He still had to return to Fairbanks, and in those short days of February, night was always a whisper away.

He was looking about anxiously for the cans of gasoline that had been promised for the refueling necessary for the return trip.

"We'll take care of that, Ben," promised one of the men. "Just you leave everything to us. We'll have the ship loaded with mail, refueled, ready to go. Meantime, come sit down to dinner with the folks."

Ben started to protest. He wanted to tell all those jostling about the vital necessity for him to find his way back to Fairbanks while some vestige of daylight still remained. But while he was still shaping the words, the crowd swarmed about and almost carried him away to the banquet that had been prepared in celebration. He was disappointed at not seeing Jasper MacKenzie. "Heading over to the Innoko River country, last we heard."

He tried to be polite and listen to the enthusiastic speeches, but his head was half turned, looking toward the river and the waiting plane. One o'clock came and the food was still heaped on the table, the speakers still droning on. Two o'clock passed and the leaden skies grew sullen, the speakers still extolling the marvel that had overtaken Alaska.

Finally risking rudeness, Ben rose to his feet and thanked those about him. He told them his one concern was how many hours of daylight were left. How would he land at Fairbanks in the darkness?

He chinned himself on the propeller, raced back to lean into the cockpit and ease the spark, but the motor failed. He tried it twice more, with an uneasy silence falling over the spectators. Finally the motor roared into action. Ben crawled into the cockpit, lifted his hand in farewell and took the ship into the air.

For an hour and fifteen minutes he bore northeast, looking from side to side as the gray clouds fringed over into black. He tried to think of the frozen land below in a detached way, as a series of landmarks carrying him toward Lake Minchumina, the halfway mark on the lonesome trip. Yet inevitably he began to speculate on his chances of survival if he should be forced by the swift onrush of darkness to land in the gloomy white expanse below. The De Havilland had a higher landing speed than the lumbering Jenny, and a swift descent from the sky to the unknown hazards of the ground could mean disaster.

But he shook the thoughts from his mind. The motor roared without faltering. If he could drive himself as faithfully as the pistons and cylinders in the mass of metal at the nose of the ship, all would be well. Another hour passed. He looked far ahead into the gloom. The bluff at Nenana should be showing. He began to distrust his judgment. Perhaps he should swing far to the right, pick up the tracks of the Alaska Railroad and follow them north to the little town at the juncture of the Nenana and Tanana rivers. But that would be additional time, and with daylight racing into obscurity, he could brook no delay. He had to pick up Nenana on a true course. He had to.

Back over his shoulder he could see the pure white crown of McKinley silhouetted against the last light of day. But down below, as he looked anxiously over the edge of the cockpit, night had overtaken the land. He was alone in the sky, without a star, with only the interminable roaring of the Liberty motor to keep him company.

He edged off course to the right, abandoning hope of picking up the lights of Nenana. His only chance now was to bore on through the darkness toward Fairbanks, keeping to what he hoped would be a straight line, trusting that those who waited for him would realize his plight and make some kind of flares.

Never before had he felt so entirely alone. He was not afraid of dying. His constant hours aloft had prepared him for such a contingency. He was regretful that the first mail flight should end in disaster, that the chance for the territory to acquire airmail service which it so sorely needed, would be snuffed out even before it was begun. And in an impersonal way, he regretted that the De Havilland should be wrecked because of his foolishness in wasting those precious hours in McGrath.

Yet he never entirely gave up hope. Through interminable hours of habit he kept twisting his head from side to side, peering down in the chill caldron of blackness before him. He nosed the ship over at intervals, scanning the dark horizon ahead, always hoping to pick up some distant glimmering of light.

Suddenly a light appeared, then a string of lights, leaping, flaring, growing stronger and stronger as he bore straight ahead to the warm golden glow.

Grinning to himself, he instinctively leaned forward and patted the side of the laboring airplane.

"Fairbanks. We're home!"

He dropped the ship low, fishtailing to kill his speed, looking anxiously at the confusing row of bonfires that had been set. He could see figures dancing about excitedly, but nothing else. The field itself was clothed in exasperating shadows. He wasn't sure of himself. Was he too close? Too far? Never mind. He had to go in. There was no choice.

He cut the motor, sitting rigid in his seat as the wind whistled by the open cockpit. Only his head twisted from side to side as he tried to find a path through the darkness down to the flickering lights.

He was startled when trees appeared directly in

front. He pulled hard on the stick, trying to lift the plane. A ski snagged. A tree branch brushed cruelly across his face. The plane spun and shattered into the ground.

Yet he remained conscious through it all. He felt himself being pulled from the wreckage. He was still alive. The first airmail flight in Alaska was over.

CHAPTER 11

Alaska was hungry for a hero, and Alaskans seized upon Carl Ben Eielson with almost ferocious paternalism. He was their Ben, their flier, their hero. With one daring, dramatic flight he had brought more favorable publicity to the northern territory than had occurred in the previous twenty years of twilight living. The amazing time comparisons between the dog-sled mail runs and that accomplished by Ben in his De Havilland plane was a newsy morsel that was seized upon and reported in most sections of the United States.

Far off in Washington, D.C., the Postmaster General of the United States asked for the attention of the President and his cabinet, and then proceeded to read Ben's official report on his first mail flight. President Calvin Coolidge, the man who was famed for a sparse use of words, promptly dispatched a congratulatory letter to the young aviator.

Ben delighted in the publicity. Although he said little when strangers stopped him on the streets of Fairbanks to congratulate him on his deeds, his step was lighter when the well-wishers had gone and he continued on to the airfield.

He was the hero of the day and he liked it.

After the battered plane was repaired, he made the second trip to McGrath and return without incident. And the third trip. And the fourth. The admiring Alaskans were confident. The ship was ruggedly dependable, even more so than the Jenny, but every time that Ben lifted the De Havilland into the air and headed southwest for McGrath, or northeast to Fairbanks, he was beset by worries. When the snowstorms came unexpectedly, he battled them high over the tundra. When fog closed about him and his ship, he worried his way through to his destination.

Once aloft, he was in a new world but always alone. There was no living person to whom he could stretch out a hand and ask for help. There was no guide book to consult, no radio to query, no beacons to guide him; even the ground markers below, changing shapes and colors with the snows, were elusive, unreliable.

Then the "good" flights were finished.

Coming into McGrath for his customary landing on the river ice, the skis of the plane ripped into the weakened covering and were broken off. Ben made hasty repairs and got home to Fairbanks where the skis were removed and the wheels put back on the plane. For the remainder of his airmail flights he landed on the gravel bar outside of McGrath.

The rains of the new spring were making the landing field at Fairbanks a quagmire—and a nightmare for Ben each time he roared in. The stiff-legged wheels seemed to reach out awkwardly as though reluctant to touch the soggy earth.

At sixty miles an hour, the landing speed of the plane, the feat had all the earmarks of driving an automobile at high speed over a shell-pocked battlefield.

The situation was bad in April. The plane flipped over on its back twice, each time sustaining injuries which were repaired only with heroic effort. One of the stories most often recounted about Ben during this period was of a passenger who had clambered in over the mailbags and settled back for the thrilling ride. At Fairbanks the thrill became too pronounced—the plane crashed on landing and nosed over, leaving the bewildered passenger hanging upside down in his safety belt.

When Ben crawled beneath the inverted plane and cut the straps, the unhappy passenger promptly fell into the mud.

The passenger patted himself tenderly, then looked from the topsy-turvy plane to the tall young flier who stood over him.

"Shucks, Ben," he said, "do you always land a plane like this?"

There was humor in the crack-ups, but uneasiness, too. Not from a sense of personal danger for Ben, but because the flights and the equipment were being watched closely by the Post Office Department.

Ben could not sleep at night for worry about men in distant places who were keeping a coldly calculating account of his airmail venture. Figures were being entered, columns totaled, results evaluated. Even while he battled head winds trying to make the home field, Ben would be worrying about the bookkeepers and their ultimate report on the McGrath-Fairbanks flying venture.

When he came into Fairbanks on the eighth mail trip in May, 1924, he felt the sudden, swiveling lurch as the wheels dipped into a soggy spot of ground. He pitched forward, slapped about the cockpit, then braced himself as the awkward ship nosed down, raised its tail on high and crashed shudderingly to the wet earth. Grimly he cut his safety straps and let himself fall to the ground.

He was already on his feet and surveying the damage when Charlie Schiek raced over from the sidelines.

"You hurt, Ben?"

He shook his head. "No—but look at the plane."

The carpenter walked slowly around the battered ship.

"The propeller I can unbend," Schiek reported. "We've done that before. And that rudder's no big problem. But Ben, those wing struts—that's serious."

Ben nodded glumly. As he wrestled the mailbags from the forward cockpit, he kept thinking of the Post Office Department. "I'll get a wire off right away. I'll tell them we'll need a little extra time before we take off on the next trip."

Schiek lifted his shoulders. "Can't tell till we try."

The report was sent in, and almost like an echo the reply came over the wires.

The contract was canceled. Airmail flights in Alaska, even though two additional trips to McGrath were still to be run, were abruptly ended. Just to make the cancellation complete, Ben was ordered to ship the battered De Havilland back to Seattle.

The letter he received from the Assistant Postmaster General, despite the praise it contained, had the same statement of finality.

"Your experiment has been successful to a marked degree," he wrote, "but there are many things which must be done before we can continue on a permanent basis our use of the airplane for carrying the mail in Alaska."

And that was it. The dream ended.

For days Ben sat alone in his hotel room. He was tempted to quit Alaska forever.

Editorially, the newspaper was shrilling indignation at the abrupt cutoff of airmail service. But Wrong Font Thompson spoke to Ben quietly. "We know you've been hurt, Ben, hurt more than the rest of us here can understand. But we want you to know—even if you never fly another plane up here—you've done something no other man ever did for us. You proved you can fly an airplane up here rain or shine, clear or blizzard, a hundred above or forty below. You've done it. And you've proved it's possible for commercial aviation to succeed up here in Alaska." He put his arm roughly on Ben's shoulder. "Come on, boy. You're young. It's not the end of the world. Get out there and do some more flying. Go see Jimmy Rodebaugh."

Already other fliers, attracted by Ben's short-lived success, were coming to Alaska.

Jimmy Rodebaugh, a conductor on the Alaska Railroad who was completely dumfounded by the difference in speed between the lumbering trains and the noisy airplanes, had transferred his astonishment into an equally dumfounding move and bought a Curtiss Standard airplane. Not able to fly himself, he nevertheless formed the Alaska Aerial Transportation Company, and proudly worked about his grounded plane.

"Ben," he exclaimed, "I'd be tickled crazy to have you fly for me. Look at this ship!"

Ben tried to hide his disappointment. Flying the Standard would be a step backward after the De Havillands. Especially when he had been dreaming of the newer, faster, planes being built down in the States, all of them with far more powerful motors and enclosed cabins for the pilot's comfort.

"And take a look at that Hispano-Suisa motor—" Jimmy Rodebaugh said excitedly. "The wings are bigger than that old Jenny you flew and she can lift five hundred to six hundred pounds!

"And you won't be flying alone, Ben," Rodebaugh continued enthusiastically. "I got a young fellow about your age from Minnesota coming up to fly—name of Noel Wien. He'll be flying another Standard up here after it gets shipped to Anchorage. We're going to be big business, Ben," Rodebaugh said seriously. "Mark my words."

Ben took to the air again, alternating flying chores with young Noel Wien. He was impressed by the young man from Minnesota, finding him quiet, methodical and a thoroughly competent flier. "Guess I'm too impatient for this job, Noel,"

Ben confessed one afternoon when they walked toward the planes that stood at the far end of the field. "Seems like I'm always on fire, wanting new and better planes—or being mad at the Post Office Department for canceling that contract."

Noel Wien hesitated before answering. "A pilot can't afford to be impatient in this country, Ben. You fly with what you got on hand. Just make sure you get back to the ground all in one piece—and those bigger and better airplanes will come along in due time. Don't try to rush things."

But Ben couldn't conceal his resentment at the Post Office Department, or his impatience with the slow, lumbering planes he was flying.

In the early summer of 1924 the two oddly contrasting fliers opened up new air trails in the northern territory, flying on diverse missions that would ultimately become the bread-and-butter occupation of the Alaska bush pilots.

The two airmen carried passengers up to Livengood and Circle and down to Kantishna, over to Poorman and Ruby and Tanana—wherever men waited, wherever clearings or river bars would accept the thin wheels of the Standards. They carried newspapers and groceries, machinery, medicine, frightened dogs and their equally frightened masters.

They literally battered new pathways across the interior of Alaska, using their chunky airplanes as battering rams to force passageways through the blue skies above the brown tundra.

They had to make forced landings by the score —so many that it became a part of the normal routine. Yet the waiting river bars took away many of the terrors of the deed. When disaster threatened, Ben nosed down for the nearest river bar. Then he would make emergency repairs—wing tips fashioned from willows then covered with muslin bought from the nearest trading post; broken wheels beefed up with spruce poles or strips from freight crates; iron patches screwed to wing spars.

Of necessity Ben also learned how to make minimum repairs to the motor so that in an emergency he could coax the engine back to life, spin the propeller and limp back to the home field at Fairbanks.

In spite of the excitement of the new venture, Ben found it impossible to forget the airmail contract. Every time he flew over a lonely settlement, he remembered the link he had forged between McGrath and Fairbanks. What had been done—even for a brief time—between those two towns could be done between others—and permanently.

Anchorage was waiting to be tied to Fairbanks in the hub of Alaska. Nome, far over on the Bering Sea, was already looking uneasily to the coming winter when the ice would block the ships from Seattle, and seven months of isolation would almost strangle the settlement. Only a few hours by plane, Juneau was, in reality, still a full week's travel by train and boat. And Seattle was an impossibility.

Airmail service, with the Government sponsoring the ships required, and paving the new airfields, would be almost a necessity if these probing, tentative hops of the little planes were to expand and cover the width of Alaska, and eventually reach down for the ultimate connection with the States.

One day Ben flew back to the field and turned the ship over to Rodebaugh. "I'm quitting, Jimmy," he said shortly. "I'm going back to Washington and fight for that airmail contract." He boarded an Alaska Railroad train and headed south to the waiting steamship at Seward.

Ben knew there would be some who would say he would never come back.

In Seattle he boarded the train and went directly across country, in his haste even by-passing a visit to his home in Hatton. He interrupted his journey only at Chicago in order to clamber aboard the Baltimore and Ohio train heading down through Ohio and Maryland into Washington.

In the shimmering heat that enveloped the nation's capital, he walked from one office building to another, trying to trace the elusive "someone" who was blocking airmail service for Alaska.

Although no one would admit to blocking airmail service, no one did anything about reviving it. Ben patiently filled out the intricate bid forms for establishing airmail service in various sections of the country. He waited impatiently while they were processed, and he fought to control his temper when, one after the other, they were rejected in favor of continued service by dog teams.

He made one last circuit of the solid white buildings baking under the August sun—then gave in to complete discouragement.

He headed west, not to Seattle and a return to Alaska, but to Hatton, North Dakota.

"Welcome home, Ben," his father said quietly. "This time I think you will stay!"

He sat morosely in the cool shade of his father's large home, enjoying the company of his brothers and sisters—but with his thoughts always on Alaska and the tiny airplanes that were buzzing the brown tundra.

He listened respectfully while his father spoke of the dangers of flying, nodding his head in agreement. There was an end to everything. Perhaps this was the end of his flying. Perhaps Alaska had all been a strange, exciting interlude, a two-year adventure that had been as unreal as a dream.

He felt as though he were standing apart, looking at himself and his father, sitting on the porch of the family home at Hatton.

In a trancelike state, he heard himself saying to the older man, "It's true. I'm going to enroll at

Georgetown University in Washington. I'm taking up law again."

He made the journey from Hatton back to Washington almost without awareness. He went through the motions of enrolling in the Georgetown University Law School—a flutter of white forms and scrawled signatures, standing in line, entering new rooms, seeing new faces, all of them swimming by in a blur of unrecognition.

He thought perhaps he was ill, yet he was reluctant to speak of the uneasiness that gripped him. He stared at his books and read nothing; he attended lectures and heard nothing. He spent one sleepless night after the other.

Ben had been at school less than three weeks when he walked into the night and continued walking until dawn.

The next day he sent a telegram to his father in Hatton.

I HAVE JOINED THE ARMY AIR SERVICE. PLEASE SEND MY UNIFORM.

CHAPTER 12

Ben was flying again but his thoughts were always about Alaska. At every opportunity he talked to his superior officers at Langley Field in Virginia. His first proposal was for the establishment of a government-sponsored flying service from the United States to China, with stops at Reno, Nevada; Nome, Alaska; Manchuria and Peking. The officers listened to him politely. They made notes on small pieces of paper, then gave the inevitable answer, "Eielson, we just don't have airplanes capable of doing that job, and if we did, the Army couldn't spare them."

But Ben was unable to restrain his enthusiasm. He countered with his second proposal. "Then," he said, "why not establish military bases in Alaska? We need those airplanes up there to repel an enemy attack."

But the answer was always the same. No planes were available.

Ben stifled his anger when he overheard an army general say, "These young fliers get carried away with their big ideas. As far as I'm concerned the airplane will never be anything more than a scouting device, a means of looking a few miles ahead of the soldiers that will be advancing on foot."

By a stroke of luck Ben was able to obtain an interview with a man who thought differently—forty-five-year-old General Billy Mitchell, assistant chief of the Air Service, a veteran flier and a man who believed passionately in the future of the airplane in the defense of America. Within a year's time, that same enthusiasm was to hurl him into a bitter controversy with his superiors, result in his court-martial and resignation from the service.

Mitchell listened sympathetically as Ben told of his crashes with the De Havilland while carrying the mail between Fairbanks and McGrath. "Nothing to that," he snapped, "only these fool nonfliers make a big to-do about it. Wasn't a week ago I flipped over in a De Havilland. Dead engine and I put it down in the Ohio River. But," he snorted, banging his fist on the desk, "I'm not giving up flying because of that!"

The General listened carefully to Ben's plans for military flying in Alaska. "I'll try, Lieutenant—but we're working against a lot of people in high places who still believe that the skies should be left to the birds!"

When Ben left him he rushed to his hotel room and wrote a letter to Wrong Font Thompson in Fairbanks:

General Mitchell is a good friend of Alaska, Wrong Font. I pointed out to him what could be done in the way of mapping, photography, gathering data and carrying government people about Alaska, and he was very much impressed.

I emphasized the fact that practically nothing has been done about Alaska where the airplane is so badly needed. General Mitchell admits this is true.

My very best regards to yourself and everyone in Fairbanks. I shall never be satisfied until I get back there.

But as quickly as Ben's hopes had flared, they died again. He kept waiting to be asked to explain in more detail his plans for airplane service to China and the establishment of military bases in Alaska.

The months raced by. The year 1924 was finished, and the year 1925 began. Ben was resigned to failure.

His term with the Air Service ended in July, 1925. Then he packed his bag and returned to his home in Hatton, North Dakota.

The thought of continued flying had become repellent to him. "Better if I had gone into some profession right after the war and stayed with it," he said to himself. "At least I'd have a job with money in the bank. Now I have neither."

He decided to turn his back on flying and accepted a position that was totally unrelated to the work he loved. Listening to the urging of his brother Oliver, he became a bond salesman for a Minneapolis firm.

For two months he traveled about the state trying to become interested in his new occupation but failing entirely. He received a letter from Wrong Font Thompson telling him that Noel Wien had brought a Fokker F-3, five-passenger airplane to Fairbanks and formed his own company, the Fairbanks Airplane Corporation. Ben tossed the letter aside. He told himself that he was not interested.

In Langdon, the county seat of Cavalier County in northeastern North Dakota, he was waiting his turn in the local barber shop when a long-distance call came for him from Hatton.

Ben rushed to the phone. His father was aging and he always dreaded the news that he might receive when away from home. But it was Ole Eielson himself who spoke excitedly to his son, his voice high-pitched and strained. "Ben," he said, "there's a telegram here for you from New York City. I went ahead and opened it."

"Who's it from?"

"That Arctic explorer Vilhjalmur Stefansson."

"What does it say?"

"He's helping a man named George Hubert Wilkins to organize an expedition to fly over the Arctic Ocean. Wants to know if you'll work for Wilkins as a pilot. Ben, can you hear me?"

Ben heard his father, but he was speechless, stunned by the swift turn of events. Captain George Wilkins was a well-known Australian who, although only thirty-seven years old, had already made an enviable reputation as an Arctic explorer. For years he had followed dog sleds in journeys through the Arctic wastes. For years he had been an ardent admirer of other Arctic pioneers like Stefansson and Amundsen—now he wanted to use this fast-developing weapon and conquer the Arctic by air.

Twenty-four hours later Ben was on the night train to New York where he signed with Captain George Wilkins to fly as a pilot in the proposed transpolar expedition.

Carl Ben Eielson returned to Fairbanks on February 17, 1926. The following day he addressed two hundred and fifty students at the University of Alaska, a few miles outside the city.

"As you fellows know, I'm a workingman, working pilot for the Detroit Arctic Expedition which is backed by the Detroit *News* and businessmen from that city. The leader is Captain George Wilkins. Most of you have heard of him from his previous accomplishments in Arctic exploration. Because I happen to know my way around Fairbanks I've been sent ahead of the group to arrange for a hangar, to hire mechanics, to see that the airstrip is smooth, things like that.

"As to the aims of the expedition—they've been covered thoroughly in the newspaper account, but I'll repeat them again. We're interested in the region lying north of Point Barrow, right on up to the North Pole—most of it unexplored.

"Captain Wilkins will be bringing up two monoplanes, one of them a tri-motor Fokker with three two-hundred-horsepower air-cooled Wright engines. The other is a smaller Fokker with one four-hundred-horsepower Liberty engine. Both of them have enclosed cabins." He smiled at the audience. "That's quite an advance over the Jenny and the De Havilland I was flying around here two years ago.

"We have about forty thousand pounds of freight to fly from Fairbanks into Barrow on successive trips. It will include twenty-five hundred gallons of gas, radio sets, men and supplies." He hesitated. "The flight from here to Barrow has never been made before. There are some mighty high mountain passes to slip through before we can coast down the other side to the Arctic slope.

"We're going to set up a supply depot by the trading post at Barrow. When that's finished, we plan to undertake aerial exploration over the ocean, a region about twelve hundred miles long and eight hundred miles wide. No living person has ever been in that region. We're lucky we have airplanes to take us in there to have a look at it.

"If everything goes well, we're going to make our first exploration flight out over the Arctic ice, look around and then get back safely to the base at Barrow. Following that, we plan another trip where we land on the ice and plant the American flag.

"Finally, if all goes well, we intend to fly straight across the North Pole and land at Spitzbergen in Europe."

Ben was waiting down by the Alaska Railroad station when the expedition rolled into Fairbanks one week later. He helped unload the five carloads of freight, unraveling the thick quilts that protected the wings of the two airplanes.

Ben tried to avoid the inevitable commotion that swirled about the expedition. He had the greatest respect for Captain Wilkins and was impressed by the Australian's dogged determination to succeed in the Arctic venture. He thought his best contribution to the success of the venture would be to work on the assembly of the two planes and to keep out of the limelight.

The smaller of the two planes, the "Alaskan," was assembled quickly. Every day swarms of visitors came out in weather that sagged to fifty-two degrees below zero. They crowded into the small hangar, hampering the work. Ben held his tongue, for most of them were his friends.

He did find a few moments to spend alone with Wrong Font Thompson. He confided to the newspaperman that when the expedition finished its work he intended to start an air service of his own down in Anchorage.

The second plane, the "Detroiter," was assembled. Ben tried to hide his disappointment when Wilkins selected Major Lanphier of the Army Air Service to take the controls for the first flight. He was sick when he saw Palmer Hutchinson, a newspaperman from Detroit, walk backward into the propeller. He was killed instantly.

It was part of a continuing series of blows to strike the Detroit Arctic Expedition. Work came to a temporary halt.

Five days later, the smaller "Alaskan" was at the head of the runway. This time Carl Ben Eielson was at the controls. Ben looked at Wilkins as he prepared to gun the motor. It was the first time he had ever flown with the leader of the expedition, and he was anxious to make a good impression.

There was a rush along the snow-covered runway. The "Alaskan" lifted into the air. When Ben turned he saw Wilkins smiling at him.

For more than thirty minutes Ben circled and glided with the sturdy ship. He was warmed by the praise that Wilkins shouted into his ears. Then, at a command from the Captain, he headed back to the runway. They came in straight as an arrow. The motor was cut at two hundred feet—and promptly stalled.

The ground leaped up to grab at the small plane. Even before Wilkins shouted at him, Ben tried to gun the motor into action and climb but it was too late. The wheels smashed into a fence surrounding the field. The screeching plane slammed ahead for twenty yards, metal crumbling and tearing. Ben and Wilkins leaped from the ship unhurt. The airplane was slumped to one side like a broken bird.

Ben bit his lips. It was a sorry beginning. He fully expected to be fired. But Wilkins, who had been hardened to disappointments, said nothing. He ordered the three-motored "Detroiter" rolled out of the hangar, and when it went aloft, Major Lanphier was at the controls.

Ben blamed himself for the crash of the "Alaskan." Already he was composing a letter of resignation from the expedition.

He was standing by the runway when Major Lanphier brought the "Detroiter" in for the landing. Ben stared incredulously when Lanphier repeated the same error he had made. The motors were cut too soon and the big ship crashed in a stall at the head of the runway.

Ill-fortune seemed to be a byword of the Detroit Alaska Expedition. Ben continued to work with the others on repairing the two broken planes. He expected any moment to have Wilkins call him aside, make a few hesitant remarks, then tell him that he was finished.

But it didn't happen. Wilkins seemed to have only one aim in life—to get the planes back into the air. If he had any doubts about Ben he kept them to himself.

On March 30th, twelve days after the accident, Wilkins walked up to Ben who was working on a fuselage of the small plane. "Eielson," the Captain said, "the 'Alaskan' is ready for a trial flight. You're going to take it up."

Ben nodded. He reached for his gloves and walked outside the hangar. When the plane had been pushed out Wilkins climbed in. Ben looked about, checked over the motor of the airplane, then eased himself into the pilot's seat.

This time everything went right. The "Alaskan" circled about Fairbanks with easy grace, and the landing that Ben made was perfect. When they were safely on the ground Wilkins turned to him. "We'll take the first plane over to Barrow tomorrow," he said quietly. "You will be at the controls."

On March 31st at seven-thirty in the morning the "Alaskan" lifted into the air. Aboard besides Ben and Wilkins were three thousand pounds of gasoline and supplies. Their course was for Point Barrow, the northernmost settlement in Alaska, five hundred miles away.

The route lay over the least-known part of Alaska.

There were no reliable maps.

There were no weather reports.

The land beneath them was just as deadly and menacing as the ice cap about the North Pole.

This flight was the beginning of a strong relationship between Eielson and Wilkins that was to outlive disappointment and bring enduring fame to both. The skills of each man matched. Together they could accomplish prodigious feats.

The plane slipped over the frozen Yukon, crabbing for altitude past Mount Doonerak, and headed through the murky fog for Anaktuvuk, a pass in the Endicott Mountains. Ben had to feel his way through the snow-covered rock wall, the mountains towering over the small plane. He had to place absolute reliance in his airplane, in Wilkins' navigation and in his own judgment at the controls.

They were whipped through the pass by a mighty tail wind. Safely through, the same wind hurled the small plane past the frozen Colville River, and over the round hummocks of the northern foothills, and down to the chalky white barrenness of the Arctic Coastal Plain. The high overhead wing stretched like that of a gull, riding easily on the wind.

Aware of his weakness for getting lost, Ben tried to memorize point by point the white wilderness over which the plane was droning. There was Lake Chandler beyond the pass, the mighty Colville River, which, even beneath its ice shield, gave promise of being a helpful marker on the future flights that would be needed along this supply route from Fairbanks to Barrow.

He was momentarily panicked by the tundra of the icy plain, unblinking below, which looked like poorly made, underdone pancakes, but he was reassured by Wilkins' evident great command of navigation.

When, after more than six hours of flying, they neared Barrow he looked expectantly at Wilkins, waiting for the command to turn into the wind for a landing at the farthest north trading post. But instead Wilkins gave the signal to continue onward.

The wind hurled the small plane far out over the frozen Arctic Ocean. When Wilkins nudged his shoulder, Ben craned his neck to look down at the rough ocean ice far below.

"No one else has ever seen that," Wilkins shouted.

Finally the Captain gave a signal to turn about. Ben leaned on the controls, dipping the wing of the plane and heading back for the Eskimo houses at the Barrow trading post. Carefully he felt his way in for a landing, letting the plane drop slowly.

The "Alaskan" was the first plane to make the hop north from Fairbanks. It was the first ever to fly over the Arctic Ocean, the first ever to touch down on the Arctic slope. The flight from Fairbanks to Barrow, with Ben Eielson at the controls, was the longest nonstop flight yet made in the Arctic.

Barrow was a tiny settlement more than a hundred years old where two stores, a native school, a mission and a hospital, grouped around Eskimo dwellings, comprised the northernmost encampment of humans in the entire hemisphere. For the greater part of its long history Barrow had been host to whalers; now it was to become an important point for airmen.

The front door of the settlement was the Arctic ice pack; its back yard was the monotonous, windswept white wilderness of the Coastal Plain. The flat frozen land was part of the United States Naval Petroleum Reserve established three years previously. The Coastal Survey had sent small mapping expeditions into the land, but most of it was uncharted, and for all purposes, Barrow stood as a midpoint between two unknowns.

Ben knew it was a focal point for bad weather, for vicious, sudden storms. He was grateful for the shelter offered by the small spot in the white wilderness; but he was not ashamed to admit his

uneasiness at the desolation hemming in the out-
post.

They were forced to wait for five days in the
trading post at Barrow until an Arctic storm had
ended. Then they made the return trip to Fairbanks,
stopping overnight at Circle City because they
were lost. Ben was relieved when Wilkins took the
blame for the error in navigation that caused the
landing.

The next freight hop from Fairbanks to Barrow
late in April was made without incident, but the return trip was accomplished with a great deal of
hazard. First a fire destroyed the canvas covering
about the motor and almost destroyed the plane
itself. Then Captain Wilkins fractured his arm spinning the propeller. It took four perilous attempts
before Ben was able to lift the "Alaskan" safely
into the air and head for home.

He was scarcely settled on the field at Fairbanks
when word came that Admiral Byrd had success-
fully flown to the North Pole and returned to his
starting point at Spitzbergen.

And the following day brought the news that
Amundsen and Nobile had piloted the dirigible
"Norge" over the North Pole to a landing at Teller,
Alaska.

It was impossible for Ben not to feel a twinge
of disappointment. He had hoped to be the first to
make the flight.

With the news of the other successes the Detroit Arctic Expedition faded quickly from the headlines. Captain Wilkins announced quietly that the expedition was finished.

"I hope to return the following year," he said to Ben. "And I want you to be my pilot again."

After a brief visit to his home in Hatton, North Dakota, Ben cast about for an opportunity to add to his fast-dwindling funds. The search led him to Florida where he spent the remainder of 1926 flying new airmail routes. It was "eating money" as he described it.

The telegram finally came inviting him to rejoin the expedition as chief pilot.

In February, 1927, he was once again back in Fairbanks. Ben led the parade of planes from Fairbanks north over the route he had pioneered into Barrow. He had been so hardened to trouble on the previous expedition that without it he was almost uneasy.

The gasoline they had so laboriously flown to Barrow during the previous year was still intact, and plans for the first long flight over the Arctic ice proceeded swiftly.

The new Stinson biplane was ready, having been remodeled just for this one Arctic task. It was crammed with extra gas tanks. The flying instruments were extensive and the best available. Looking over the array, Ben could not help thinking of his early days of flying, ten years before, when a string tied to the wing of his plane was his only indication of adequate air speed. Now he marveled at the compass, the tachometer, the oil-pressure gauge, the oil thermometer, the air-speed meter, the altimeter and the bank-and-turn indicator. Added to those standard instruments was the special navigation equipment Captain Wilkins had insisted upon—an aperiodic compass and an earth-inductor compass, a drift indicator and a course-and-distance calculator. Tucked inside the crowded fuselage was a special sounding gear they would use when landing on the ice to determine the depth of the Arctic Ocean beneath.

Wilkins was ready.

Ben was ready.

He lifted his hand in signal. The wheel chocks were withdrawn and the heavily laden ship took off for its epic exploration over the Arctic ice. For five and one half hours the two men were triumphant in flight as they roared into the northwest.

Then the engine began to miss. Ben placed the ship into a glide, reached for the ice and landed safely. He leaped out and hurried to check the engine. With equal haste, Wilkins rushed to take a sounding of the depths of the waters beneath them.

For two hours Ben worked over the engine. He ripped off the cowling and the carburetor as he sought the source of trouble. The temperature was thirty degrees below zero. He wondered uneasily what would be their fate if he were unable to start the engine again. Finally they climbed aboard. The engine responded. The two men tensed as the ship raised on the rough ice and lifted into the air.

But they were aloft for only ten minutes when the engine failed again. Once more they brushed close to death as the plane lurched to the uneven ice. Once more Ben sweated over the engine, his fingertips freezing solid.

They were aloft again, this time in total darkness. The fuel gave out. The plane for the third time headed down toward the ice in the darkness below. For twenty minutes it floated downward in the quiet darkness.

CHAPTER 13

Skis touched, bounced, lurched and crashed. Then there was a sudden silence, the weird song of wind whistling through the wires that braced the wings of the Stinson biplane.

Eielson bent over the controls, exhausted. George Wilkins leaped out of the plane and in the darkness ran his hands over the skis. The metal splinters that gouged his fingers told him what he had refused to believe. He climbed back into the plane, racing to escape the blizzard. The two men looked at each other. With a sudden convulsive twitching of muscles they began to laugh. Then the thought of their escape from death sobered them. Without a word, they unrolled their sleeping bags and turned in.

Between them and the mainland were ninety miles of gigantic ice fields cut and chewed in an endless earthquake. The temperature was far below zero.

When they woke from their sleep the wind outside the stranded plane blew at thirty miles an hour, driving a fine snow before it. To Ben it was a reminder of the winter blizzards in his home state of North Dakota. To Wilkins, always practical, calculating, it meant that starting shoreward over the ice was impossible for that day.

He clambered out of the ship, chopped a hole through the flinty ice and dropped a weighted line to ascertain the drift of the flowing ice.

"What is it?" Ben asked.

"The flow is moving away from the shore line." Wilkins shook his head. "Every hour we're going to be six miles farther from help at Point Barrow."

It was as though a man walking from Philadelphia to New York had the ground under his

178

feet shifting westward in the direction of Pittsburgh.

Ben shook his head in disbelief.

Wilkins readied the provisions they would carry, biscuit and chocolate and army emergency rations—thirty-eight pounds in all. Most important were two Mannlicher .256 rifles with four hundred rounds of ammunition. "Hope I don't get a chance to test my theory," Wilkins said, smiling slightly.

"What's that?" Ben asked.

"That two men can live on the Arctic ice for two years with only three hundred and fifty cartridges. We'll see."

The second day Ben and Wilkins were still prisoners in the crippled plane. The wind whistled with a menacing sound. But they were not idle. They improvised two hand sleds: one from the tail ski, the other from the lower part of the cowling. Ben never questioned Wilkins' authority or his knowledge. Once he remarked, "Should we leave a message in the plane in case a rescue party finds it?"

"There won't be any rescue party," Wilkins answered. "I left written instructions to that effect before we took off from Barrow. Those at the base will have returned to Fairbanks by now." As far as the world was concerned, they were dead. In the columns of the Detroit *News,* the paper that had spent so much money on the expedition, they were already slipping off the front page into oblivion.

Another day went by while they waited for the wind to ease. It wasn't until the sixth day that they started to walk out of the tomb that held them. Their task was to cover the ninety miles of drift ice back to the invisible shore line, then to continue westward along the bleak ocean front back to the trading post at Barrow.

On the first day away from the plane, they traveled for five hours, hauling on the small sled, floundering through drifts of wind-driven snow that were waist-high.

That night they built a snowhouse, slicing the blocks expertly, canting the edges a fraction, building the mound row by row until the center cap was on. Despite his years in Alaska Ben had never before seen a snowhouse under construction. He helped mortice the crevices with soft snow even though his frozen fingers were swollen and tender. The snowhouse was solid against the wind—and warm.

They talked little, but at one point Wilkins remarked, "I measured our drift when we crossed that open lead today going west. We might miss Barrow."

For five days after leaving the plane they tramped and floundered and crawled. They traversed a hideous collection of ice, broken and crumbled into fragments, some of them as small as Ben's fist, still others the size of a house. There were open

180

leads that must be skirted and long snow bridges that must be crossed.

After a long winter of immobility the ice was beginning to move slightly. Every movement of the current added to the chaos on ice. Wherever open water showed, a rising cloud of steam hung in the air. The horizon about them was punctured with steam clouds, and in the sharp clear atmosphere the clouds took on the shape of fortresses, hemming them in.

They were tiring, so they concentrated their dwindling load of food and essential supplies on one sled, pulling it with rawhide thongs as they scrambled forward. Ben's frozen fingers were blackened and tender. The smallest finger on his right hand blistered, causing him continual pain. He saw Wilkins watching him nervously, and he sensed that the older man was debating a halt while he performed a surgical operation and cut off the finger. Ben was glad when Wilkins' courage appeared to fail, and they went on.

There were bear tracks and fox tracks all about them, but not once did they see any game. Even the seals were missing from the open leads, and that, more than anything else, worried Wilkins. His entire theory of two years survival on the ice depended on seals. "The bears hunt the seals," he explained to Ben, "and the foxes eat what the bears leave. Scavengers—they travel together." He looked up at the gray sky. "Gulls, too."

On the tenth day while they inched forward, the ice began to grind, floes in the open leads tumbling and shrieking like stricken animals as they crushed against each other. Huge bergs tumbled and crashed together, the crunching noise and the sharp pistol cracks carrying with startling clarity in the deathly still air. Ben held back, watching as the ice floes hammered, squeezed and rammed against each other in a chorus of unearthly screeching.

"If this keeps up," Wilkins said grimly, "these floes will be shredded like ice going through a machine. We can't waste any time getting to shore." They decided to abandon the sled, take on their back what was left of the food, and press forward. Even the sleeping bags were abandoned, though Wilkins decided to keep only the lower half of one, to be used to shelter their feet at night.

The ice before them was spread out in fantastic confusion, jagged ridges sometimes fifty or sixty feet in the air. It was impossible to skirt the ice rubble for it was endless, stretching to either side as far as they could see. They were forced to their hands and knees, crawling, counting a hundred yards as good progress for an hour. They rested face down on the ice. Every time Ben's hand touched it, he winced with pain.

Wilkins explained to Ben the terrific upheaval

182

of ice meant they were nearing the shore. The old floe ice was grinding and tearing itself on the shore ice firmly anchored to the mud bottom of the shallow ocean.

Then Wilkins' legs began to swell. It must have been agony and Ben admired his grim-faced courage and his superb confidence.

They came upon a fifty-foot lead of open water anchored to the far side only by a thin bridge of spongy ice, most of it already under three or four inches of water. A detour might mean a delay of days while they skirted the lead, and even one additional day could mean the end of their endurance.

Staggering with fatigue, Ben plunged forward. He pulled up sharply when the ice sagged beneath him, the water lapping within a fraction of the top of his boot. He recoiled, scampering back to the secure edge.

"I'll try it," Wilkins said.

Ben watched as the older man started across, legs shuffling awkwardly, the ice pick held outstretched like a band instrument. Almost across the ice bridge, within a few yards of the far side, he turned to nod encouragement to Ben—and at the same moment plunged waist deep into the icy water.

Ben stifled an exclamation of horror. He started to run forward to help Wilkins when he saw the Captain, with one convulsive movement, heave himself out of the water to the ice bridge, then roll over and over to the firm ice.

Ben sucked in his breath slowly. Even from a distance he could see that Wilkins was soaked through. And the temperature was ten degrees below zero.

He knew that the accident could mean death for both of them. The water trickling from Wilkins' boots was already beginning to turn to slime. The wet clothing, with terrible swiftness, would become an ice shield.

But Wilkins slipped out of his heavy pack, then tossed a line over to Ben and pulled him across the ice bridge to the firm ice on which he stood.

Ben looked at the Captain sharply. He knew if a man were to give up the fight to live it would show first in his eyes. "Better keep moving," he said to Wilkins. "I remember listening to people in Fairbanks—"

But Wilkins was looking about expectantly. Ben realized that a man with wet clothing in sub-zero temperature rolls himself in deep, soft snow which acts as a blotter soaking up the excess water. But on the windswept ice there was no snow.

Wilkins jumped to his feet and ran stiff-legged to some rough ice that sheltered him from the wind. Ben lifted the packs and hurried after him. The two of them pulled off Wilkins' stiffened boots and socks. As best they could they squeezed out the excess water in his clothing. Then Wilkins pulled on dry socks and boots that were in the pack. He jumped to his feet and ran about in short circles, his arms flapping comically. Yet there was no smile from Ben, who was watching. He knew that Wilkins' life hung in the balance.

Now, more than ever before, there could be no turning back, no stopping.

Wilkins slung his pack on his back and started forward. "We've got to keep going before my blood turns to ice," he said. "Never been so cold in my life."

Their stop that night was a miserable experience. The pain in Ben's finger kept him from sleeping even though he was exhausted. And he could feel Wilkins shuddering in his wet clothing.

Four days followed, each worse than the last. The closer they approached the shore, the more terrible became their struggles. A full hour of rugged progress brought them only the length of a football field.

The amount of food they consumed was negligible. They wanted only to get off that broken ice on which they were the sole living creatures. It was an area from which even bears and foxes had retreated.

On the seventeenth day of their ordeal Captain Wilkins and Ben hauled themselves over the last pressure ridge. Ahead, as far as they could see, was an unbroken expanse of smooth shore ice and flat tundra. They collapsed on the bank, shivering with exhaustion, but triumphant.

The next morning they started westward on the one-hundred-and-fifty-mile trek to Barrow, hobbling eagerly like returning soldiers, then resting. Hobbling and resting.

Although they were alone at the top of the world, they had escaped the first sentence of death. They were off the ice.

"But it was another failure," Ben said dispiritedly.

"It was no failure," Wilkins snapped. "We proved that it was possible to make forced landings on the pack with an airplane, didn't we? We proved that strong men could get out of the pack even without dogs, didn't we? It was no failure."

Their conversation was interrupted. In the clear Arctic air they heard the yelping of sled dogs. Looking up, they saw a native and his team bearing down on them. Ben felt like sitting down and crying. When they returned to the hospital at Barrow, his finger was amputated.

CHAPTER 14

The night after the operation Ben was restless. A throbbing pain ran from his finger, through his arm and over his shoulders. He slipped into his parka and walked out into the cold Arctic air, where he stood quietly in the light snow, shivering slightly. Dimly outlined in the darkness were the ridges of the ice pack over which they had recently crawled to safety.

He wondered if he would have the courage to start out again on the transpolar flight should Wilkins ask him. What was the good of it all? Wilkins kept repeating that they were blazing a trail which one day would be used by commercial planes flying from America to Europe over the North Pole. Could it be true? Two lonely men battling disaster and disappointment in the Arctic—doing something for the future of the world? It didn't seem likely.

The pain in his finger eased and he nodded sleepily. When he turned to go back into the trading post, he looked across the Bering Strait toward Russian Siberia. Then he retraced his steps back to the trading post, dark in the moonlight.

Ben waited impatiently until a relief plane was sent from Fairbanks for him and Captain Wilkins. But disaster still dogged them. On the return trip they ran into a series of difficulties. A cylinder blew out of the engine, forcing them to make an emergency landing at Wainwright. After painstaking repairs the plane limped back to Fairbanks.

There was a wild welcome staged for the two returned airmen. It flared up quickly—and died quickly, too.

Further treatment was necessary on Ben's finger and the doctors forbade him to embark on any long flights in the near future. Wilkins tried to get under way with another pilot—and the effort failed. Finally, fighting his discouragement, the Captain declared that exploration for that season had ended.

They returned to Seattle where Ben was paid off. He looked ruefully at the money in his hand. Exploration paid little money. He had earned more teaching school in Fairbanks five years before.

But he turned cheerfully to a proffered position as an inspector for the Aeronautical Division of the Department of Commerce, confident that Wilkins would find another financial backer and that the two would be heading north again before too many months went by.

Wilkins was on fire with an ambition, to fly from America to Europe over the North Pole; and Ben knew he would never rest until that ambition was accomplished—or the brave airman was dead.

Late in 1927 Ben received a letter from Wilkins which bubbled with enthusiasm for a new type of airplane he had just seen. "The most beautiful thing I've ever looked at," Wilkins exclaimed in his letter. "No wires, no exposed controls—nothing but wing and this streamlined fuselage! A Lockheed Vega, they call it, and I'm hurrying down to southern California to see Allen Lougheed, the builder."

Ben grinned when he read the letter. He knew that, by some miracle, Wilkins would be able to raise the money to buy the plane. And he was right.

In the next letter Wilkins said, "Lougheed is building a plane for me—the third to come out of the factory. I'm positive I'll be able to go north again, and this is an official offer to you to accompany me as chief pilot on the flight from Point Barrow in Alaska to the island of Spitzbergen in the Greenland Sea, six hundred miles north of the tip of Norway."

Ben never hesitated. He obtained leave from the Aeronautical Division and took a train for Los Angeles.

Wilkins was waiting to greet him. "Ben," he said excitedly, "you've never seen anything so beautiful in your life as this little airplane."

They drove through the streets of Los Angeles

in Wilkins' old automobile to the Western Air Express Field on the outskirts of the city of Glendale. There in a small hangar Ben had his first view of the plane that would carry him on the third attempt to conquer the Arctic ice.

He tried to restrain his enthusiasm for the trim, bullet-shaped monoplane. It seemed to him to be imbued with life, poised and confident, as though conscious of its ability to perform with ease prodigious feats in flying history. "She's all right," he said quietly. "I'll know better after I take her up."

He took the machine off carefully and landed with even more care. Then he went up again and again. Deliberately he punished the plane, twisting and turning it, inviting disaster. If it must come, let it be here, on the proving grounds of southern California rather than over the pack ice in the Arctic.

The plane answered every command.

As though they would never be entirely free of trouble, however, the ship, when only one hundred feet in the air on one of the take-offs, suddenly stalled and nosed down for the ground. Ben banked it sharply and managed to flatten out for a rough landing in a plowed field. Wilkins, who had been following in a car, ran over to the plane. He was white-faced. "That was nearly the end of the expedition," he said. "What happened?"

Ben shook his head.

All through the night they labored over the engine, helped by Allen Lougheed and Jack Northrup, the designer of the plane. They found the cause of the motor failure, and it was remedied quickly.

From then on, Ben and Wilkins drove out to the field in Glendale every day and flew the machine. Ben lost count of the number of times he took off and flew over the dry Los Angeles River and the wheat fields of the San Fernando Valley. Hourly his love for the sleek machine increased. He became even more enthusiastic than Wilkins. "This ship will do it," he said emphatically. "She'll take us across."

Wilkins was delighted with several innovations in the small airplane, especially with a glass panel that had been installed in the floor. From this he would be able to observe while taking sights for ground speed and drift. In the other planes he had been forced to look out into the wind, suffering from cruel exposure.

On the third of February, 1928, the two men parted temporarily. Wilkins was to see to the arrangements for shipping the plane north. Ben went ahead on the Southern Pacific train to Seattle where he was to spend several days with his father and his oldest sister Elma, who had journeyed from their North Dakota home. While the train crept through the San Joaquin and Sacramento valleys, across the border into Oregon, and then into the state of Washington, he had ample opportunity to review his life since the time he had flown his first plane nearly ten years before. The only part he regretted was the time he had turned his back on flying to work as a bond salesman.

This time Ole Eielson didn't try to persuade Ben to give up the Arctic flight. "It is your life—flying. I accept it. I pray now for your safety and your success." Ben's sister wept quietly when she kissed him good-by.

On the trip north from Seattle to Seward in Alaska, Ben and Captain Wilkins practiced sending the International Code. Their plane would be equipped with a radio, and they hoped to be in continuous touch with Barrow during their flight across the top of the world.

They arrived in Fairbanks on the evening of Sunday, February 26th. The few people who met them were far from enthusiastic. Wilkins' expeditions in Alaska up to this time had been associated with disaster and failure. But Ben's loyalty to the Captain was unshaken.

"Sure," he admitted, "we've had bad luck. But it can't continue. This time we're going to make it."

On the morning of March 19th they rolled the Lockheed Vega out of the hangar, lined up with the runway and raced into the air. The flight over to Barrow, on the path Ben had pioneered, through the Anaktuvuk Pass in the Brooks Range, was made without event, the small plane performing beautifully. While they were greeted warmly by the ones who had helped them so often in the previous years, no one really expected the expedition to succeed.

For three weeks they were busy in the sub-zero temperature at the trading post, preparing for the long flight. Most of the time was spent in carving a fourteen-foot runway through the snowdrifts down which the heavily laden plane must thunder before taking to the air.

Scores of natives were hired, provided with picks and shovels and set to hacking out the long, narrow trough down which Ben would guide the plane.

When he did try it for the first time, the ship veered sharply to the right, crashed into the snowbank and crumpled one of the skis. Disaster still dogged the expedition.

On Sunday, April 15th, after the metal skis had been replaced with wooden ones, Captain George Wilkins finally pronounced the expedition ready to depart. He went out early to the plane, and Ben followed, lugging the engine oil in cans wrapped in a double sleeping bag to keep the heavy fluid from freezing.

He poured the oil into the engine, looked about briefly, then climbed into the forward section of the fuselage.

Ben sat alone in the pilot's seat. Wilkins climbed into a tight compartment behind him where the navigating equipment was installed. They were to be separated for the entire flight; only a small speaking tube led from one section to the other, though Wilkins was able to pass notes up to Ben.

Wilkins waved his hand in signal. The natives grasped the wings of the Lockheed Vega and wiggled them violently, freeing the skis from the grip of the slick snow.

Ben gunned the engine. The natives pushed forward and the ship moved slightly. Then, motor roaring, the heavily laden ship picked up speed as it skidded down the narrow runway, the wing tips within inches of the snowbanks on either side. Ben tried not to think of it. An error of just one foot to the right or the left would send the plane screaming into the snowbanks. Fire would be inevitable. In the tight quarters, he knew that it would be impossible for either Wilkins or himself to escape.

His grip on the controls was firm. At the right moment, when the snowbanks were dropping behind with blurring speed, he sent the plane into the air. The little ship responded valiantly, inched slowly upward past the restraining grips of the snowbanks and into the dark blue sky.

The cluster of houses at Barrow flashed beneath them, then dropped behind. Once more the two men were over the Arctic ice.

Ahead of them, if they were successful, was one of the most difficult long-distance flights ever attempted up to that time. Ahead of them, if they failed, was almost certain death.

Ben kept the ship climbing until it reached an altitude of three thousand feet. Then he leveled off in flight, following the invisible line Wilkins, as navigator, sketched across the unknown areas. The Arctic shores of Alaska and Canada would be off to the right, and the jumble of islands lost in the ice above Baffin Bay, and then the mighty island of Greenland. Their destination was the fist-sized island of Spitzbergen, twenty-two hundred miles away.

Ben shook his head in disbelief. Twenty-two hundred miles. And it was less than five years since he had first lifted the lumbering Jenny into the air over Fairbanks!

Wilkins, from his rear navigating compartment, passed written notes to Ben regularly, telling him what course to follow. The compass could not be trusted. They were in a weird spot where every direction tended to be north, as though anchored firmly to the top of the earth. And they were coming closer and closer to the mysterious, magnetic North Pole, that odd region which takes hold of a compass needle and forces it far to one side of true north.

At times it was necessary to change course

every few minutes to correct for the compass errors. Only the sights which Wilkins took of the sun were reliable guides.

The motor droned on faithfully hour after hour, a loud, comforting sound that Ben relished. From force of habit he swiveled his head about constantly, checking on all sides, even though he had nothing but dark blue sky above and an ocean of ice below. The ice fields of the Arctic were a white desert, far more desolate than the tundra of interior Alaska which had been broken at times with clumps of thin-boled trees. Here there was nothing.

Hour after hour the plane roared on through the cloudless blue sky. They were in the air for ten, twelve, then thirteen hours.

Wilkins scribbled a note and sent it forward. Ben read the message. "If you look ahead, you can see the mountains of Grant Land. If you wish, we can make a landing there and walk overland to a Canadian Mounted Police Station on Bache Peninsula. Or we can take a chance on the weather and try to reach Spitzbergen. Which will it be?"

"Spitzbergen," Ben shouted back through the speaking tube. Then he reached down and pulled out one of the sandwiches from the paper bag.

He was curious, looking down at the mountains of Grant Land, for he remembered that it was from this lonely spot that Admiral Peary had finally made his successful dash to be the first man to the

North Pole. He chewed thoughtfully on the sandwich, thinking of the difference between Peary's dog-sled trip and this present one. Then he remembered his own escape from death on the ice, and he attacked the sandwich with greater vigor.

Sixteen hours after the take-off they saw dimly in the distance a peak that marked the ice-covered island of Greenland. The air grew terribly cold. Vast cloud banks rushed down upon them.

The plane nosed down and bucked wildly, but Ben held tight and eased the ship downward, seeking escape under the cloud bank. But when he approached the water, the wind took savage hold of the ship and tried to shove it into the sea.

Frightened, Ben lifted the plane high again into the region where the snow swirled in thick layers. He was blinded, and there was no escape. The eighteenth hour had passed and still the storm buffeted. The nineteenth passed, then the twentieth. Very soon they would be out of gas.

A mountain peak loomed perilously close out of the swirling white clouds that engulfed them. But by its base was a flat, snow-covered area. Ben circled out to sea, then fought back against the raging wind to a landing on the snow.

So fierce was the wind that the plane was scarcely moving thirty miles an hour when it touched to the surface. Immediately Wilkins leaped out and pulled himself, stiff-legged, to the engine where he started to drain the oil. This was necessary to prevent it from freezing within the motor block.

At the same time he shouted to Ben, but the latter, deafened by the day-long pounding of the motor, could not understand what he was saying. Finally, in answer to Wilkins' wild gestures, he grabbed the engine covers and leaped out to fight the canvas covers about the engine. The two then huddled out of the wind in the tiny navigating compartment.

"We're close to Kings Bay on Spitzbergen," Wilkins said. "Very close. Perhaps less than an hour's flight away. But I'm not sure exactly where we are."

When the wind lulled for a few minutes, they drained the gasoline from the tanks and decided the twenty gallons remaining were sufficient to carry them to safety at Kings Bay—if they could find it.

But when they were about to take off again, the storm blew with renewed fury. For five wearisome days the two men were prisoners in the storm-buffeted airplane.

When they did try to go aloft again, it was necessary for Wilkins to stand outside the airplane, shoving hard against the fuselage to free the tail skids and skis from the grip of the freezing snow while Ben got the ship rolling. Wilkins was still outside the ship when Ben took off, thinking the

Captain had crawled safely inside the fuselage. But Wilkins had been unable to pull himself forward against the nightmare tug of the wind, and had dropped back into the snow. It was not until Ben was aloft that he circled and saw Captain Wilkins waving frantically at him.

Once more Ben landed the plane on the narrow strip. Once more it was necessary for Wilkins to stand half in and half out of the plane, shoving and pushing while Ben got the ship under way. This time the Captain managed to hold on and pull himself in while Ben took the ship into the air.

They were scarcely aloft and clear of the mountaintops when Ben yelled and jabbed his fingers downward. Far to the side were two radio masts and the open pit of a coal mine. Quickly Ben put the ship into a glide and landed at the foot of the radio mast. Men on snowshoes started hastily down the slopes toward the plane.

For Ben Eielson and Captain Wilkins the journey was ended at Green Harbor on Spitzbergen Island.

They had flown from Alaska to Europe, across twenty-two hundred miles of Arctic ice and snow, a distance in these high latitudes that was halfway around the world. Fifty per cent of that area had never before been seen by man. They had been aloft for twenty hours and twenty minutes.

That night, with the help of the powerful radio

199

transmitters at the coal mine, the world knew of the successful flight. Ben Eielson's name was flashed into every corner of the world, linked to that of Lindbergh and Admiral Byrd.

He was now not only Alaska's hero but the nation's hero, as well.

CHAPTER 15

The wireless word of their accomplishment that flashed around the world set in motion events which seemed to reach out like fingers and take hold of Ben and Wilkins, carrying them along swiftly as though they no longer had control of their own movements.

They boarded a ship that took them to Norway. Then throughout all of Europe it seemed there was no honor too great for them. The people of Norway, Denmark, Holland, Germany, France, England—all acclaimed the two fliers.

Ben was awarded the Lief Ericson Memorial Medal with inscription: TRANSPOLAR FLIER OF NORWEGIAN ANCESTRY FOR VIKING DEED IN DARING. And he watched with gratification as Wilkins, the Australian, knelt before George V of England and knighted, becoming Sir George Wilkins.

There was a brief time of rest while they crossed the Atlantic Ocean by boat until they stepped ashore at the pier in New York. There they were accorded a hero's welcome.

Ben flew the Lockheed Vega cross-country to North Dakota where he landed in the same hayfield at Hatton from which he had once flown his Jenny. Everybody, so it seemed, in the state of North Dakota had turned out to greet the return of the hero, including the governor of the state, who was waiting with outstretched hand as Ben climbed from the plane.

There was music and excitement, pressing throngs and Ben was utterly nonplused that such a terrific demonstration should have been staged by the usually staid North Dakotans. He was overwhelmed by the demonstration. This was a hero's welcome, and all he wanted was to be an old friend.

He was reluctant to leave the plane. As he stepped into the crowds, he looked back over his shoulder at the Lockheed Vega. "No," he said, in answer to questions, "it wasn't much of a trip from Alaska to Spitzbergen. I just sat in the plane and steered it and went where Wilkins told me to go, and that's all there was to it."

He was not being consciously modest. It was impossible for him to forget how much he owed to the navigation of George Wilkins.

He spent a few weeks resting at home waiting for word to come from Wilkins. Once more the daring Australian was launched on another intrepid scheme. Because of the favorable publicity resulting from the Arctic flight, he was able to line up financial backing for another proposed exploration trip, this time at the bottom of the world, across the Antarctic wastes.

Less than two months after he had returned home to Hatton, Ben was off again. Wilkins' Antarctic Expedition would have two Lockheed Vega planes, one of them the old favorite that had carried them across the northern wastes.

They sailed south from New York into the Gulf Stream, around the nose of South America, touching at Rio de Janeiro and finally at Montevideo in Uruguay. There they transferred to a Norwegian whaling ship which took them far south to Lonely Deception Island.

When the Lockheed Vega plane was put ashore at the island, it was the first ever to reach the Antarctic continent. Bad weather hung over the party day after day and it was not until November 22, 1928, that Ben was able to make his first Antarctic flight.

When Ben returned to the base after the first test hop, the wireless operator rushed up to him excitedly waving a paper. It was a message from Washington saying that Ben had been awarded the Congressional Medal of Honor for his part in the flight from Alaska to Spitzbergen across the top of the world.

Striking out from Deception Island a few days before Christmas, Ben flew the little plane for twelve hundred miles. He and Wilkins sighted six unknown islands. They were the first men to fly into the Antarctic, the first to discover land from the sky in that desolate region. Then the weather closed in on them and the brief period of exploration was over. They sailed north again on the *Hektoria.*

They were in Chile on February 15, 1929 and in New York City a month later. Once again there was a gala reception by the mayor's committee and once again Ben was escorted to City Hall where Mayor Jimmy Walker officially welcomed him and Wilkins. He was no sooner resting at home than he received word he was to come to Washington, D.C., to accept the Distinguished Flying Cross from the Assistant Secretary of War. The Assistant Secretary said Ben's flight of the previous year from Alaska to Spitzbergen "was one of the most extraordinary accomplishments of all time."

On April 9, 1929, he returned to Washington for the second time and President Herbert Hoover presented to him the Harmon Trophy for the most outstanding feat in aviation for the year 1928. Charles A. Lindbergh had been the recipient on the previous year for his nonstop flight from New York to Paris.

But now Ben had greater plans in mind, and they all involved Alaska. It was as though the country was a lodestone. Little else interested him. He wanted nothing so much as to return to Alaska as the head of his own aviation corporation.

He spoke to a group of bankers in New York. "We're past the creeping stage in Alaskan flying," Ben assured the financiers. "We're ready to start running all over the face of Alaska—running with the fastest, finest planes we can get. But we need money to get started—a lot of money from people like yourselves who have confidence in the future that is awaiting Alaska."

It wasn't an easy victory, but Ben's persuasion, together with the solid accomplishments of his own flights, won over his audience. They agreed to furnish the money for planes, pilots, mechanics and bases that would enable Ben Eielson to set up in Alaska a passenger and freight network.

Back in Fairbanks, Ben brushed aside all efforts of his friends to continue the plaudits that had greeted him ever since the flight across the top of the world. "I'm a businessman," he said. "I'm not interested in parades. I want to get airplanes into the air."

He was authorized to buy out the Fairbanks Airplane Corporation that his quiet-speaking friend Noel Wien had started three years before. And into the fold of the new corporation came the air service that excitable Jimmy Rodebaugh had started even earlier. Ben made no effort to hide his plans for the new company. "We're going to cover Alaska," he said flatly. "We're going to service every town that can offer us freight, passengers and a landing strip."

Business for Ben's new company was brisk and his planes were flying continually. One day, late in October, word came that an American trading ship, the three-masted *Nanuk*, was icebound off the village of North Cape, Siberia. Aboard her were fifteen passengers and one million dollars' worth of fur pelts. The market for furs was sagging. Each day the furs remained locked aboard the ship meant a tremendous loss to the owners. They offered Ben fifty thousand dollars if his company would airlift the cargo and passengers from the ship and ferry them to Alaska.

Despite his former intention to stick mostly to "desk flying," Ben decided to participate actively in the task of salvaging the furs aboard the *Nanuk*. He selected as his mechanic twenty-eight-year-old Earl Borland. Earl, who was married and the father of two small children, had already been marked by Ben as a young man who could go far in the organization.

The practice of carrying a mechanic along on most flights was rapidly taking hold in Alaska bush flying. Not only were they of inestimable use when the inevitable forced landings occurred, but they "doubled in brass" as freight handlers, propeller spinners and emergency relief pilots.

The ship Ben piloted was a single-wing Hamilton cabin plane, snug and tight against the winter storms, its all-metal finish seemingly impregnable to the buffeting of the Arctic winds. It could carry eight passengers or, with the seats removed, a well-paying load of freight. It was fast, sturdy, ideal for the job it was being called upon to perform.

Ben flew due west five hundred and twenty-five miles to Nome, refueled and rested, then took off for the sixty-mile flight almost due north to the rough landing strip at Teller on the Seward Peninsula. There was a roadhouse which would serve as a meeting place for pilots, for he had called in several of the company planes to participate in the airlift from the winter-locked trading vessel.

He stood by the plane for a few moments as Earl Borland adjusted the cover over the motor and drained the oil from the crankcase. He looked west to the Bering Strait. Far beyond, around the bulging snout of Siberia that pressed close to Alaska, was the *Nanuk*, three hundred air miles away.

As though to prove how easy it was to earn the fifty thousand dollars, the next day Ben made the first of the scheduled trips out to the vessel. He landed on the ice by the ship, helped Earl load up with six passengers and one hundred thousand dollars' worth of furs, and headed back to Teller. The weather forced him to make an emergency landing by a Siberian village. But three days later, when the storm eased, Ben easily lifted the plane over the Bering Strait to the safety of Teller.

Then a blizzard howled down from the north. Day after day the assault continued. Day after day Ben and the other flyers, whom he had summoned to assist in the fur-salvage venture, stood in the Teller roadhouse and looked up impatiently at the storm-clouded sky.

In that first week of November, about the sixty-fifth degree of latitude, there were only five hours of daylight, four hours of murky twilight, then a long night of fifteen hours. And the daylight was disappearing. Within two weeks the daylight hours would be gone entirely, and the night would be black for eighteen hours, followed by six hours of an uneasy twilight that made for dangerous flying, and necessitated suicide take-offs and landings.

Impatience finally overruled all the caution Ben had acquired in six years of Arctic flying. On the morning of November 9, 1929, he called over his shoulder that he was leaving for a flight to the *Nanuk* despite the weather. Earl Borland, his mechanic, rose to his feet and accompanied him. They climbed into the plane. The propellers tore savagely into the wind as the ship headed into the storm.

The hours passed without word. Then the day became night, and the people of Alaska knew definitely that Ben's ship must be down in the Arctic.

The days turned into weeks with no sign of the fliers, and the greatest aviation search in history up to that time was launched. Hope held high because of Ben's previous escape from death in the Arctic. Men were sure that once again he would walk to freedom.

November passed and the search planes fought their way through storms in fruitless ventures. As December passed, hope for Ben's rescue ebbed.

On January 27, 1930, seventy-nine days after the disappearance of Eielson and Borland, Alaskan pilot Joe Crosson landed his search plane by the *Nanuk* and held aloft a piece of twisted metal. When he came aboard, he said, "We found Ben's plane. He crashed in Siberia."

Two weeks later the bodies of Carl Ben Eielson, aged thirty-two, and Earl Borland were uncovered from the mounds of snow that encased them. The altimeter of the plane had been faulty. They had flown into a hillside and been killed instantly.

Eielson's name lives in an Alaskan mountain, Mt. Eielson, that towers in the shadow of Mount McKinley.

And just outside Fairbanks is Eielson Air Force Base, home of the 5010th Air Base Wing. By the entrance to the base is a monument to Ben with the inscription:

FATHER OF ALASKAN AVIATION AND AIRMAIL SERVICE. FIRST TO FLY AN AIRPLANE AROUND THE NORTH POLE FROM ALASKA TO SPITZBERGEN.

Daily, huge bombers on weather reconnaissance lift from the runways of Eielson Air Force Base, fly north over the Brooks Range, over the frozen Arctic Ocean, to circle the North Pole and return, following the invisible path blazed by the boy from North Dakota.

Almost hourly jet fighters from the same base roar into the sky over Fairbanks in ceaseless patrol that protects not only Alaska, but all of the United States far to the south.

And daily from airports at Los Angeles and San Francisco huge commercial airliners roar northward, over the tier of states into the wilderness of northern Canada. High in the sky, they follow the Eielson trail across the top of the world, over the Polar ice fields to Greenland, then streak onward to Sweden, Denmark and Germany.

Each flight is a tribute to a man who gave his life to make it possible, the greatest Alaskan flier of all time—the beloved Carl Ben Eielson.

BIBLIOGRAPHY

Andrews, Clarence L., *The Story of Alaska*, The Caxton Printers, Caldwell, Idaho, 1938.

Herron, Edward A., *Alaska: Land of Tomorrow*, McGraw Hill Book Co., New York, 1947.

———, *Dimond of Alaska, Adventurer in the Far North*, Julian Messner, Inc., New York, 1957.

———, *William Healey Dall: First Scientist of Alaska*, Julian Messner, Inc., 1958.

London, Jack, *The Call of the Wild*, The Macmillan Company, New York, 1903.

Mitchell, General William, U. S. Army, *Skyways*, J. P. Lippincott, New York, 1930.

Potter, Jean, *The Flying North*, The Macmillan Company, New York, 1945.

Rolfsrud, Erlind N., *Brother to the Eagle*, Lantern Books, Alexandria, Minnesota, 1952.

Wilkins, Captain George H., *Flying the Arctic*, Grosset & Dunlap, New York, 1928.

INDEX

Aeronautical Division, Department of Commerce, 188-89
Alameda County, 11
Alaska, 38, 41, 42, 44, 46-88, 89-135, 136, 137-58, 159, 161-64, 165-75, 179-80, 188, 192-95, 199-200, 201, 203-9
Alaska Aerial Transportation Company, 155-58
Alaska Hotel, 76, 86, 91, 100, 154
Alaska Railroad, 47, 59, 86, 102-3, 105, 107, 111, 115, 140, 147, 154, 158, 167
Alaska Range, 106
Alaska, University of, 165
"Alaskan," the, 167, 168, 169-74
Aleutian Islands, 47
America. See United States
Amundsen, Roald, 165, 174
Anaktuvuk Pass, 171, 193
Anchorage, Alaska, 58-65, 86, 106, 157
Antarctic Expedition, 202-3
Army Air Service, 38-42, 145-63, 168
Arctic Coastal Plain, 171-73
Arctic Ocean, region of, 165-75, 176-86, 187, 189-90, 192, 194-99, 206-9

Arctic Slope, 127
Australian, 35, 165, 201-2
Aviation Section, United States Army Signal Corps, 1-20, 24-29, 79, 141

Bache Peninsula, 196
Baffin Bay, 195
Baltimore and Ohio Railroad, 137, 158
Bartlett Glacier, 56
Bering Sea, 42, 47, 157
Bering Strait, 187, 206-7
Berkeley, California, 24
Berlin, Germany, 36
Birch Creek, 130
Black Wolf Squadron, 38-42
Borland, Earl, 205-8
Brooks, Alaska, 126
Brooks Range, 127, 129, 193, 209
Byrd, Admiral Richard E., 174, 200

California, 1-20, 22, 24, 26-29, 31, 56, 84, 91, 189-91
Canada 38, 42, 82, 195, 209
Capitol Building, 44, 137
Cavalier County, North Dakota, 164
Chena Slough, 71, 85, 88, 95, 96, 97, 102, 112, 118, 123, 133, 140

Chicago, Illinois, 35, 41, 128, 136, 158

Chile, 203

Chilkoot Pass, 68

China, 14, 161, 163

Circle City, Alaska, 113, 130-31, 156, 174

Circle Hot Springs, 131

Colville River, 171-72

Congressional Medal of Honor, 203

Coolidge, President Calvin, 150

Crosson, Joe, 208

Crumrine, Lieutenant, 40

Curtiss JN-4 planes, 4, 10, 15-21, 25-27, 31-38, 82, 83, 89-120, 121-35, 141, 146, 150, 166, 195

Curtiss Standard plane, 155-58

Cushman Street, 73

Dawson, Alaska, 51, 68

Deception Island, 202

De Havilland planes, 38-42, 79, 129, 139-54, 155, 162, 166

Denmark, 200, 210

Detroit Arctic Expedition, 165-86, 188

Detroit, Michigan, 165, 168

Detroit News, 165, 179

"Detroiter," the, 168-69

Distinguished Flying Cross, 203

Eielson, Adeline (sister), 21

Eielson Air Force Base, 209

Eielson, Arthur (brother), 21

Eielson, Carl Ben, as air cadet, 1-21, 24-29; ancestors of, 2; his friendship with Hank Robinson, 3-4; his navigation poor, 3-12, 13-15; childhood and youth, 21-22; family, 21-22; attends college, 22-24; passes flight check, 27; is transferred, 29; is commissioned, 29; enrolls again at college, 30; is restless, 30-31; gives flying instruction, 33; joins flying circus, 33-37; flying becomes second nature to him, 34-35; traces route of Black Wolf Squadron to Alaska, 42; walks away unhurt from plane crash, 43; studies law, 43-44; works as Congressional guard, 44; meets Alaskan delegate, 44; his friend Hank dies, 45; takes teaching job in Fairbanks, 45; his trip to Alaska, 46-54; with Jasper Mackenzie, 49-50; is delayed, 57-71; as a teacher, 74-75, 83; is asked about flying in Alaska, 78-79; will be pilot for new company, 81-83; tries to learn surrounding terrain, 84; realizes difficulties in winter flying, 85-86; his airplane order acknowledged, 86; his plane finally arrives, 89; tests it in flight, 94-98; his first commercial trip, 102-6; stunts for spectators, 109-11; takes passengers on sightseeing trips, 112-15; performs for President Harding, 115; makes delivery to mines, 116-18; lands despite obstacles, 119-20; flies by compass, 122-23; makes Alaskan history, 123-24; gains confidence, 127; his dreams,

212

127-28; writes Government about need for Alaska airmail service, 129; learns to be mechanic, 132; receives rejection from Post Office Department, 134; visits his family, 135-36; sees Sutherland in Washington, 137; is told he will fly Alaska's first airmail route, 139; worries about getting lost, 140; now flies a De Havilland, 140; has skis put on plane, 140; his first airmail flight, 143-49; is Alaska's hero, 149-50; receives congratulatory letter from President, 150; continues flights through storm and fog, 150; comes through other bad landings 151-53; worries about Post Office Department's reaction to costs, 151; his contract canceled, 153; is tempted to leave Alaska, 154; flies for private firm, 155; opens up new air trails, 156-57; makes emergency repairs, 157; fights for renewal of Alaska airmail, 158-59; gets nowhere, 159; studies law again, 160; joins Army Air Service 160-63; talks with General Billy Mitchell, 162; becomes bond salesman, 164; is to pilot for explorer Wilkins, 165; will be flying unexplored Arctic region, 166-67; on first Arctic expedition, 168-75; his Alaska-Arctic firsts, 173; flies new airmail routes in Florida, 175; on second Arctic expedition

with Wilkins, 175-86; his finger amputated, 186; works as aeronautical inpector, 188-89; joins Wilkins in California, 189; tests new plane, 190; on North Pole expedition, 192-99; is national hero, 200; his honors, 200, 203-4; receives hero's welcome in North Dakota, 201; joins Wilkins' Antarctic expedition, 202-3; interests bankers in Alaskan aviation, 204; establishes new company, 205; tries to salvage furs from icebound ship, 205-7; is not heard from, 208; his body found, 208; memorials to, 209-10

Eielson, Elma (sister), 21, 22, 191-92
Eielson, Hannah (sister), 21
Eielson, Helen (sister), 21
Eielson, Olava (mother), 22
Eielson, Ole (father), 9, 22, 24, 31, 135-36, 159, 164-65, 192
Eielson, Oliver (brother), 21, 136, 164
Elliott Bay, 48
Endicott Mountains, 171
Engineer Creek, 113
England, 8, 35, 200-1
Europe, 23-24, 128, 167, 187, 199, 200

Fairbanks Airplane Corporation, 164, 205
Fairbanks, Alaska, 44, 47, 51, 58-60, 62, 63-64, 66, 71-102, 104, 107, 109, 111-15, 120-21, 123-128, 132-35, 136, 139-43, 144, 145, 146, 147, 148-58, 162,

213

163, 164, 165-70, 174,
175, 179, 184, 188, 192,
195, 204-5, 209

Fairbanks High School, 44-
45, 47, 49, 71-72, 73-76, 83

Far North, 46, 93

Farnsworth, Ira, 89-94, 100,
109, 130, 132, 134-35

Farthest North Airplane
Company, 98, 101, 111,
136

5010th Air Base Wing, 209

Florida, 36, 175

Fokker planes, 164, 166

France, 2, 8-9, 14, 15, 23-
25, 29, 108, 200

Front Street, 96

George V, 201

Georgetown University, 44,
137, 160

Germans, 7, 36; Germany,
200, 210

Glendale, California, 190-91

Gold Rush days, of Alaska,
44, 46, 47, 51, 63, 68

Goldstream Creek, 103, 113

Goose River, 4

Grand Forks, North Dakota,
22-23

Grandview, Alaska, 56

Grant Land, 196

Green Harbor, 199

Greenland, 195, 197, 210

Greenland Sea, 189

Gulf of Alaska, 52-53, 125

Gulf Stream, 202

Hamilton cabin plane, 206-8

Happy Creek, 113

Harding, President, 107, 115

Harmon Trophy, 203-4

Harpers Ferry, 137

Hatton, North Dakota, 9, 21-
22, 32-33, 135-36, 158,
159-60, 163, 175, 201-2

Havana, Cuba, 36

Healey, Alaska, 107

Hektoria, the, 203

Henriques, Ed, 39

Hispano-Suisa motor, 155

Holland, 200

Holy Cross, 108

Hoover, President Herbert,
203

Hopkins, Mr., 77-78

Hopkins, Tad, 75-77

Hutchinson, Palmer, 168

Immelmann turns, 32, 109

Innoko River country, 145

Inside Passage, the, 49

International Code, 192

Jenny, the. See Curtiss JN-4

Juneau, Alaska, 47, 80, 124,
158

Junkers plane, 128

Kansas, 83

Kantishna, Alaska, 156

Keller, Mr., 47, 59, 63, 74,
87

Kentucky, 136

Kings Bay, 198

Kirkpatrick, Lieutenant, 40

Kitty Hawk, 82

Knik Arm, 61

Kuskokwim River, 63, 141

Lake Chandler, 172

Lake Kenai, 55

Lake Michigan, 136

Lake Minchumina, 144, 146

Langdon, North Dakota, 164

Langley Field, 161

Lanphier, Major, 168, 169

Liberty motor, 39, 41, 139-
41, 143, 147, 166

Lief Ericson Memorial Medal, 200
Lindbergh, Charles, 200, 204
Livengood, Alaska, 113, 156
Lockheed Vega plane, 189-91, 192-200, 201-2
London, England, 36
Los Angeles, California, 35, 189, 209
Los Angeles River, 191
Lougheed, Allen, 189-91

McGrath, Alaska, 77, 79, 138-39, 141-46, 148, 150-53, 157, 162
Mackenzie, Jasper Jay, 49-72, 77, 145
Madison, Wisconsin, 24
Manchuria, 161
Mannlicher rifles, 179
March Field, 2, 29-30
Marin Peninsula, 7
Marne, Battle of, 9
Maryland, 158
Matanuska Valley, 66
Mather Field, 1-5, 12-21, 25-30, 91
Minneapolis, Minnesota, 164
Minnesota, 4, 30, 155
Mitchell, General Billy, 162-63
Model Café, 100
Mojave Desert, 27
Montevideo, Uruguay, 202
Moose Creek, 113
Moose Pass, 56
Mount Doonerak, 171
Mount Eielson, 209
Mount McKinley, 67-68, 143, 147, 209
Mount Susitna, 60, 61, 65
Muir, John, 47
Munson, Alaska, 117

Nanuk, the, 205-8

Nenana, Alaska, 64, 70, 90, 101-11, 115, 138-40, 143, 147
Nenana Canyon, 70
Nenana River, 106, 147
New York, 22, 35, 38, 128, 164-65, 178, 201, 202, 203, 204
News-Miner, the, 78, 111-12
Nobile, Umberto, 174
Nome, Alaska, 42, 47, 49, 51, 80, 123, 124, 157, 161, 206
"Norge," dirigible, 174
North American continent, 68
North Cape, Siberia, 205
North Dakota, 2, 3-4, 21-23, 49, 68, 76, 86, 164, 178, 191, 201-2, 209
North Dakota, University of, 22-24, 30-31
North Pole, 127-28, 166-67, 171, 174, 187, 188-89, 195-97, 199-200, 209
Northern Commercial Company, 73, 97
Northrup, Jack, 191
Northwestern, the, 48-54, 88
Norway, 189, 200
Norwegian, 2, 200, 202

Oakland, California, 5-13
Ohio, 136-37, 158
Ohio River, 162
Oregon, 192
Orteig, Raymond, 35
OX-5 engine, 19, 109, 122, 128, 141

Pacific Ocean, 11
Paris, France, 35, 36
Peary, Admiral, 196-97
Pedro, Felix, 51
Peking, 161

215

Pennsylvania, 137
Philadelphia, Pennsylvania, 178
Pittsburgh, Pennsylvania, 137, 179
Plummer, Captain, 12
Point Barrow, Alaska, 166-67, 170-75, 178, 179, 180, 186-87, 189, 192, 193-94
Poorman, Alaska, 156
Portal, North Dakota, 37, 41
Post Office Department, 129, 134, 137-39, 149-50, 152-54, 156
Potomac River, 45
Prince William Sound, 53

Red River, 4
Reno, Nevada, 161
Resurrection Bay, 53-54
Richardson Trail, 48, 81, 112, 115
Rio de Janeiro, 202
Riverside, California, 29
Robinson, Hank, 2-4, 15, 17, 18-19, 26, 27, 28-30, 31, 33-45, 53, 56, 74, 78, 90, 91
Rodebaugh, Jimmy, 154-55, 158, 205
Rodgers, Calbraith P., 22
Roth, Mr., 116-20, 121-22
Ruby, Alaska, 156

Sacramento, California, 1, 8, 17
Sacramento Valley, 191
St. Michael, 123
St. Patrick Creek, 113
Salchaket Slough, 123
Salt Lake City, Utah, 33
San Fernando Valley, 191
San Francisco Bay, 6, 45
San Francisco, California, 35, 209

San Joaquin Valley, 26, 191
San Jose, California, 7-8
San Pablo Bay, 6
Santa Cruz, California, 8
Schiek, Charlie, 140, 153
School of Military Aeronautics, 24
Seattle, Washington, 46-48, 58, 74-75, 88, 135, 157-59, 188, 191-92
Seward, Alaska, 47, 50, 59, 62, 80, 86, 88, 107, 125, 135, 158, 192
Seward Peninsula, 206
Siberia, 187, 205, 206, 208
Signal Officers' Reserve Corps, Aviation Section, 29
Sitka, Alaska, 124
Skagway, 68
"Sleeping Lady, The," 60
Smith, Esther, 74, 87
South America, 202-3
Southern Pacific Railroad, 191
Spads, 14
Spencer Glacier, 56
Spitzbergen, 167, 174, 189, 195-96, 198-99, 201, 203, 209
Sponheim, Hannah, 74, 87
Steel Creek, 113
Stefansson, Vilhjalmur, 164-65
Stewart and Denby mines, 116, 120-21
Stewart Creek, 116-21, 123, 125, 135
Stinson biplane, 175-78
Stinson, Eddie, 128
Streett, Captain, 38-40
Susitna River, 67
Susitna Valley, 67
Sutherland, Dan, 44-46, 137-39
Sweden, 210

Takotna River, 144
Tanana, Alaska, 156
Tanana River, 72, 75, 97,
    103-4, 106-7, 110, 112,
    123, 143, 147
Teklanika River, 106
Teller, Alaska, 174, 206-7
Thomas, Harvey, 9-12
Thompson, Wrong Font, 78-
    84, 89-90, 92-93, 99-100,
    115, 125, 154, 162-64, 168
Trail Creek, 56
Traill County, 4
Turnagain Arm, 60

Unalakleet, Alaska, 123
United States, 24-25, 32, 38,
    42, 79, 80-82, 107, 125,
    129, 135, 136-39, 149, 155,
    158, 161, 187, 205, 209
United States Naval Petrole-
    um Reserve, 173
Uruguay, 202

Valdez, Alaska, 47, 48, 59,
    112, 124
Valdez Glacier, 51

Virginia, 161

Walker, Mayor Jimmy, 203
Washington, 192
Washington, D.C., 38, 44-46,
    129, 137-39, 149, 158-60,
    203
Western Air Express Field,
    190-91
White Pass, 75
Wien, Noel, 155-57, 164
Wilkins, George Hubert, 165-
    75, 176-86, 187-200, 201-
    3; is knighted, 201
Wisconsin, University of, 24,
    30-33, 43-44
Wood, Dick, 78-83, 84, 87,
    89-90, 98-99, 101-6, 108,
    111, 116, 121, 127-29
World War I, 1-21, 23-28,
    141
Wrangell Mountains, 123-24
Wright brothers, 82
Wright engines, 166

Yukon River, 51, 72, 75, 108,
    123, 171